ALIVE
AND
WELL
...ONLY BLEEDING

ALIVE
AND
WELL
...ONLY BLEEDING

G.K.

XULON ELITE

Xulon Press Elite
2301 Lucien Way #415
Maitland, FL 32751
407.339.4217
www.xulonpress.com

Unless otherwise indicated, Scripture quotations taken from the King James Version (KJV) – *public domain.*

Paperback ISBN-13: 978-1-66285-475-0
Ebook ISBN-13: 978-1-66285-476-7

FOR MY BROTHER

PROLOGUE

Mid-March 2002

"Do you mind?" she asked. But her fingers were already running through his hair, lifting it ever so slowly, letting it fall, again . . . once more. If he hadn't taken her wrist, sternly removing her hand, she would surely have drawn too much attention. And a circle of drunken coeds amused at his expense was not something he could embrace as even mildly entertaining.

She was off in a huff, and Baker Faraday rubbed away the sting of her slap. Back and forth along his whiskers, he pondered whether he might want to go back to wearing a beard, let it grow out enough to match his long satin-brown hair. At least that way he might present a rugged-enough appearance to keep the presumptuous sort away—women who would ask if they could stroke it, to see if it felt as soft as it looked.

He began to feel trapped inside a room falling in on itself, pressed close to the bar by the wave of humanity that brushed and bumped past, yelling drink orders from over his shoulder. He watched as another throng of giggling girls came out of the bathroom, pinching their nostrils to make sure the cocaine stayed upstairs. From the shadows, they twirled their *own* hair, waiting impatiently until their mistaken sense of greatness could reinflate.

Spring break was a time when most Key West locals went underground, until it all blew over. But Baker had been cajoled into joining the fray, thrown headlong into the petty concerns and superficial diatribe of singles small talk. He watched as the bartender stabbed straws into the signature strawberry daiquiri, the coconut-shell rum-runner, sinking from view each time the Cuervo girl drifted by with a flirting invitation to pour yet another upside-down margarita.

He sat quietly, with one hand cradling his ale. From under a listless brow, he observed his smashed friends as they moved across the dance floor. Beside the light of incandescent tiki torches, they swayed with strangers to the broken-record seaside music like they had just arrived, able to erase that "same ole" feeling of being lifetime locals, something Baker could not shake.

All he wanted to do was get his mind off the fishnets that hung above his head as he jiggled the cord to jostle the plastic marine replicas caught in them. Baker wanted to shove the drunks and the low-hanging papier-mâché parrots out of his way and find the exit.

The desire to drive home and pick up his guitar was resolute, to participate in the one regular regimen that always provided an escape from reality, playing in intimate stolen moments before the party came looking for him, to pull him back out, putting him again in the position of the dismayed onlooker as his friends partook in one last round of sugar-laced drinks and piss-poor but oddly successful pickup lines.

They'll know where to find me, Baker thought as his tattered sandals heel-toed off the main drag, down a darker side street, crushing wind-displaced grains of sand underfoot. He raised his head slightly to sniff the heavy air, the fresh muskiness that warned of a storm approaching. Baker picked up the pace. He turned the last corner and pulled out his keys. He spun them around his finger, catching them in his palm, once, twice, before stopping in his tracks, seeing keys weren't necessary.

Parked under an arc lamp, Baker saw the door hanging open. The light cast down upon two boys who were taking liberties with the possessions inside. One was under the dashboard, his skinny dark legs dangling out the door. The other was supposed to be keeping watch but only stood outside looking in, urging his partner to hurry it up.

As Baker witnessed the thievery from afar, his body fell into a swayback posture of defeat. Another would have looked to call the police, but the small-time musician only considered his blue Ford pickup and his Taylor acoustic, which sat upright and vulnerable in the passenger seat, causing a rush of concern that a composition of almost everything of value he had could be lost in a matter of seconds.

As he approached, it began to rain, growing more intense with each step toward his truck. His heartbeat quickened as the heavy drops on broad tropical leaves concealed his advance, allowing Baker to move closer, closer still.

Before him, he saw the undeveloped bodies of children. Such an appearance gave Baker more confidence as he silently cut the distance to within ten feet of his vehicle. He stalled to regain his composure, trying to hide his legitimate cynicism toward the young thieves. Wanting only to startle the boys into taking flight and leaving everything behind, Baker bellowed in a tough guttural tone, "What do you think you're doing?"

The lookout shook in surprise. Turning his attention to the gruff voice, he quickly stepped back, the desire to flee reading plainly in his expression. The other slid out of the driver's side until his feet touched the ground, slowly standing upright with his back to Baker, holding the guitar case at his side.

"Drop what you've got and turn around, kid."

The boy's eyes were blank, his dark face taut and hard, void of youthful innocence. His bony framework could be seen clearly through the dampening T-shirt that began to cling to his body like another skin.

Baker rotated his gaze up once again when lightning struck, revealing plainly a swelling expression of hatred so strong that it riveted him to where he stood. He suddenly could no longer feel the pelting rain on his head as a barbed pang of fear coursed through his veins, dousing his confidence under what was now a deluge. Baker's blood left his face as he realized in gross misery that he had lost control of the situation, if he'd ever had control at all.

The boy would not relinquish the guitar. The gravity of the standoff intensified, and it rocked Baker into a nervous shift. He cursed his own careless nature for putting himself into such a dilemma, one that now predicted only a negative outcome. That's all he remembered before the flash.

He didn't feel the shots right away, as Baker stood motionless, watching the white soles of the boy's sneakers rapidly tread off into the night. But blood droplets soon developed into an accelerated flow, cascading freely onto the wet pavement.

Baker fell to his knees, reaching for his side, where he found a sticky cavity made by one bullet's path. A thunderclap shook the ground as more blood collected at his feet, instantly blending and thinning into the swift flow of the weather's watercourse. And with the stroke of another lightning bolt, Baker began to feel the painful jolt of the second shot. From where the throbbing pulse came, he did not want to look as terrifying thoughts raced through his crazed mind. It was all he could do to hold his hand out into the downpour and open his eyes to the sickening sight of a far greater wound.

The storm created a no man's land, an outdoor environment reserved for drunks and fools. It lashed out in the rhythm of a tragic eulogy, keeping locals and partygoers alike inside, in wait for the tempest to subside.

Huddling under a canopy, they had heard a noise, two short bursts that in no way resembled the boom of thunder. It had come from the direction of where they had parked. Upon taking inventory of their company, they noticed Baker wasn't there. And the warmth of dread melted across each of their faces, leaving only one hope in their rapidly sobering minds, a plea that just this once, he hadn't bugged out early toward the origin of those gunshots—to find his truck, go back home, and play his guitar.

1

ALIVE AND WELL

Fraser, Colorado; June 2007

For Baker Faraday, while being so high above the haze of the inner city, the moon possessed a profound presence as it illuminated the deserted street in a waft of pale blue. Such a quiet and reflective moment overtook any tension the last twelve hours had created. Yet he couldn't settle into such an exceptional instance of peace, not until he could settle the pain. So he walked.

Keep moving, he thought in practice. The movement divided tasks within his head, putting less emphasis on the discomfort.

Burn out all that is useless and impure.

Like an exercise, the walking and conscious meditation worked, most of the time.

The suffering cleanses me.

He saw these words as a slogan at first, but as he embraced these new thoughts, Baker learned to channel the negative.

Command past circumstance.

God provided the ability of Baker's free will to direct the divine pattern. So Baker reached for the disciplined intelligence He had instilled. Baker had been broken down. But he would fight not to curse what had befallen him.

Baker relived his past each time the arthritis stabbed back to reclaim weakness. After all, his easy path to blame was always a choice at the crossroad, which always appeared smooth and wide. And it tapped him on the shoulder incessantly. But like muscle, faith needed exercise in order to strengthen. So with one thoughtful rock at a time, Baker endeavored to cultivate enough of his mind to build the bulwark against what he tried to leave behind. And as Baker questioned former beliefs, he found that defeating irrational pessimism became easier. The bona fide pain was another matter entirely.

Since the shots rang out nearly five years ago, Baker had worked incessantly on the mining of his soul. His findings became his therapy, a continuing effort to rightly think, and such an ongoing revelation ennobled him, saved him, almost always.

But even the most diligent seeker can find pitfalls in the progress. The affliction in his left hand had intensified with age, able to get a foothold on his senses all too often. At its worst, Baker was no match. Only then would he seek his pill cocktail of Tolectin and Demerol, which was always close at hand. For years, he had remained careful to avoid addiction, though there were telltale signs, cryptic messages of need Baker could not notice, not from the inside.

Soon he would be thirty, with a body just beginning to lose its recuperative powers of youth. Demerol knocked back what ailed him, but how long could he use it? What he now cherished above all was intimacy with the Creator. The drugs were providing pain relief, but they also presented a barrier, rising high against any semblance of spiritual or cognizant thought. For this, under the eyes of the Lord, he felt piously taxed and void of a place to hide.

Such a situation represented an absurd paradox. His hand was throbbing after hours of playing his Stratocaster, after taking part in the livelihood he loved with an unrelenting passion. And this night had presented a bit of good fortune, hinting to Baker and his band that their trip out of Denver and away from the ordinary may have been worth it. The day had been arduous, littered with doubt, but with one show behind them, they were halfway home, leaving what they hoped was a lasting impression in their wake.

Baker followed the broad flood of moonbeams down to the parking lot, fixing his gaze on Jimmy's trailer. It sat in an out-of-the-way corner, now empty and abandoned until tomorrow night, when he and the rest of his band would call upon it again. Baker grabbed his shoulder with his good hand, to rub a trace of nagging soreness away—a feeling brought about by heaving speaker cabinets the size of coffins in and out of that ominous hollow trailer, to be fed again as soon as the gigs were over. The bothersome irritation was nothing compared to the arthritis, and laughably, it was a welcome sensation, reinforced each time he participated in the routine work of being a small-time musician.

For this misunderstood band of Christian rockers, gigs were few and far between. Desperately, they sought out a home for their music. If they had to go deep into the mountains to spread their message, then so be it.

The morning unfolded as could be expected. Nat had been late, as usual, and Jimmy, long ago dubbed "The Mole" for his preference of darkness and an overall subterranean life, was in his basement, still sleeping off a late-night *Star Trek* marathon. Murphy worked, in effect, for free on the soundboard and wasn't expected to pack up for gigs, leaving the extent of the loading to Baker, Dolf, and a rather-lathered Moby, who pissed and moaned about the no-shows the entire time.

They had a diagram taped to the inside door of the trailer, depicting how everything needed to fit, though the years of filling and unfilling left little use for the frayed instructional, serving as nothing more than a lone memento of their early beginnings.

Baker had stacked the final amplifier snugly into the rear of Jimmy's trailer when Nat arrived and pulled over the curb between the gilled fenders of his lime-green '79 Plymouth. He wore a silk shirt from the night before and a pair of sweatpants that were too short to be his, a telltale ensemble of an evening with another lady friend. He casually strolled up to his mates with duffel bag slung over his shoulder, smiling wide in his catching good-natured way. "Ready when you are, fellas."

Nat offered Moby a greeting with a firm dap handshake, affectionately draping his arm over his friend's shoulder, dousing Moby's percolating ire as only Nat's influence could. Jimmy, however, would not get off so easily. Moby already had big plans for *his* morning wake-up, which would involve a black Magic Marker and a toothbrush mustache on Jimmy's upper lip.

Upon Murphy's noontime arrival, they took their positions of travel, a subconscious arrangement that was road tested by miles of experimentation, an ongoing case study in conflicting and concordant personalities. Dolf and Moby, who wasn't allowed near Jimmy after his morning prank, accompanied Nat. They maintained enough following distance so as to avoid the plumes of exhaust that spit from Jimmy's struggling Ram Charger. Murphy read Colson in the back seat. Baker leaned over on the armrest of the door, staring out the window, daydreaming. He chose to lose himself in thought rather than fall victim to the frustration of their speed. For miles, they crawled along at the unsettling pace of a wagon train, pulling the crammed trailer through canyons, over mountains. They pulled off briefly along a stretch of two-lane road, allowing an unabated advance of the growing procession of tailgating motorists.

Moby held up his finger. "Wait for it. Wait for it . . ."

"Outta the way, Jesus freaks!" yelled an angry youth from the window of a Subaru Outback. With an unkempt beard and nest of hair, he accentuated his point with his middle finger shooting skyward.

"Ahhh, yes," said Moby, rather satisfied, interlocking his fingers behind his head, "I give you the perpetually annoyed neo-hippies of Boulder, Colorado."

"Whatever happened to peace and love?" posed Nat, scratching his head.

"I better not see him at the top of this mountain," said Dolf with nose flared, eyes growing psychotic. "He would stand a good chance of being knocked off."

"Easy, my man," said Nat. "He ain't worth it."

Trying to appease his dejection with reason, Nat continued. "Now, why's that boy so angry anyway?"

"Oh, it might be the new bumper sticker on your car, Nattie."

"Awww, man! Naw, Mobe, what does it say?"

"Don't worry, you'll love it, bruh."

As the group waited for Dolf to carelessly relieve himself, roadside, of his morning coffee, the panoramic view atop Berthoud Pass offered a pleasant diversion, its magnetic attraction pulling each of them out of their vehicles. Only Jimmy declined the invitation to gawk at the scenery. He remained behind the wheel, gazing unabashedly at his sulking face in the rearview mirror, cussing Moby under his breath as he wiped with concentrated intensity at his ink-stained upper lip.

As for Nat, he hunched behind his Plymouth, clawing at a bumper sticker that read, *God Bless Rush Limbaugh.* Murphy bent down to help.

"I told Moby, man. Nothing political, that's not how I roll."

"He knows, Nat. That's why he slapped it on." He paused. "At least it's not as bad as the last one."

"Ain't that the truth, shoo. *Coon Hunters for Christ.* That tops 'em all."

By late afternoon, they arrived at their destination. And shortly upon taking in the surroundings, the six elements of the Christian rock band Alive and Well launched into the drawn-out matter of humping each piece of equipment into the Crazy River Saloon. It was the pillar of nightlife and the only place to go for music in Fraser, Colorado. It was a place stuck in time, a place where there was nary a concern to grow past the bantam description of "quaint"—a long way to go for a gig, but the band was desperate for work, just happy to jam in front of strangers once more.

Now alone, Baker Faraday welcomed the solitude. The efforts of the last twelve hours had broken him down mentally and physically. As he strolled through the empty streets of Fraser, he listened with intent to the distant yelp of coyotes, the accompanying bugle of the elk as they pierced the darkness in disjointed song. The coyotes sounded nothing like the television reenactments Baker had come to know from a childhood spent under palm trees rather than Ponderosa pines. It came off more as if the howl were being fabricated, spun in reverse on a wobbly turntable as a misshapen portrayal from a mutant hybrid. And the elk devotedly completed the symphony in a tone analogous of a chatting clan of whales. Feeling fortunate to be within earshot of such an untamed opus, Baker rubbed his hands together, chuckling at his novice knowledge of mountain life.

His steps took him to the windows of the saloon. Looking in, Baker noticed Bear Foster, the bar owner, quietly mopping up the remnants of ash and spill. Curiosity compelled him to enter, to bombard him with questions, wanting to know what he might have thought of Alive and Well's first night's performance. But Baker had been around long enough to realize that to pursue such an answer would seem a bit too amateur, too desperate. He resolved to stand for a moment outside the window, watching the one responsible for his latest gig set chairs on the tables, clearing a path for his sudsy mop.

Bear was turning out to be refreshing temporary employment. Baker had noticed that, while he poured drinks from behind the bar, he paid attention to the music. He drank a few, to be sure, but the manager who imbibed on a simple shot now and then was a pleasant change from the municipal preferences of coke and ecstasy. Baker had a low opinion of these self-professed drug-induced monarchs of the music scene, as so many reveled in their position of being the first and last word as to who got a job on their stage—and who didn't. And at night's end, it was all Baker could do to shuffle off and find the keeper of his well-deserved pay, fighting the disgust he felt every time he had to take it from their cold and clammy fingers, swallowing hard whenever they cleared the cobwebs long enough to ask what that "Jesus" stuff was all about. After the general comment that the band would do better to drop the Bible beats, Baker would feign a thanks for the opportunity to play. While, inside, the leader of Alive and Well would fight back the impure thoughts of malice bubbling up in his mind.

If Baker, as a practicing Catholic, had one shortcoming, it was that he wasn't much on forgiveness toward those who hindered his band's advance. With a character forever under construction, he would allow his opinion to descend low enough to chasten their apathy from within, scoff at their routine choice for a drug-induced state of mind.

Alive and Well had their good nights and bad, but they always took solace whenever the person responsible for putting them onstage was into it. That alone would forever matter. It was only a sour reality to Baker and the others that they had to travel so far to find it, to a town called Fraser, an area that only reserved space on the map due to the recognition that it stood as the next community west of the Winter Park ski resort.

The storefronts were beginning to appear as all too make-believe, similar to scenery ripped from a Hollywood set of an old Sam Peckinpah film. Baker turned and walked behind the town, just to make sure it was all not a bevy of facades, pushed up by stagehands in readiness for William

Holden's grand entrance. But there were no cameras, no Holden. As if upon an empty canvas, his imagination pumped out visuals at a retarded speed, against the non-happenings of Fraser in the dead of night. The overall patience of mountain life formed a vacuum around him. And Baker felt something was missing. Just then, he noticed a set of railroad tracks running through the back of town, and as if magically conjured, a train approached.

Baker closed in as two Southern Pacific engines passed. With arms outstretched, he pressed his chest to within feet of the drawn freight. His stare remained fixed forward, looking at the full moon as each passing car eclipsed it for just a moment.

It wasn't going super-fast, just seemed faster in his turtle-speed state of mind. Baker knew he could have easily jumped it, but where would he end up, Glenwood Springs, Grand Junction, Salt Lake City? As the succession finally passed, he was left to ponder that question, as well as what had ever happened to the red caboose.

Baker bent over to listen to the tingle of the rails, when he heard gravel crunching underfoot, a loose version of "Summertime" blowing from what he knew to be a mottled patina-ridden Hohner Chrometta 8 harmonica.

"Whatta ya know, Cecil?" greeted Baker, without turning.

The band's biggest groupie took his hand from the harp, grabbing Baker's sore shoulder for a kind rub.

Gazing over the mountain plains, Cecil drew the hood of his sweatshirt off his head and returned to his tune. The night's light spread a distinct imprint across his face. An over-hanging forehead cast a shadow over his deep-set eyes. Cecil wore a nose that sat off to the left, and his protruding jaw was darkened with what seemed a perpetual two-day stubble. He was six foot five, lanky but wide in the shoulders. His clothes hung off his body as they would on a closet hanger. Not one to own any insight of the Gap's latest summer line, Cecil was sure to have attire worn by another if not more.

He often assumed a gravely sincere pose of a person one might not want to fuck with. But to the one who faithfully knew him, Cecil's physical traits paled in comparison to what made him truly fascinating. Far more intriguing to Baker was the fact that he rarely spoke. His phonetics simply flowed through his actions, his bottomless well of music. Gestures and tunes took the place of words with the utmost economy, conveyed simply in a slight smile or accented note, a forceful shove or stressed riff if he felt it necessary. It took a willing-ness above social curiosity as well as a good grasp of music history to understand these mannerisms. But once he com-prehended, Baker couldn't help but become fond of him.

The way Cecil functioned served as the ultimate counter-part to Baker's own deliberate nature. Their souls were drawn together, making them instant friends. The rangy, quiescent loner was like no other, considered saintly to the leader of Alive and Well, the one who took the time to understand his peculiar but pleasing way.

Once the tracks had retired to the repose of a whisper, Baker felt the pull to journey on. Without the need to voice his intention, Cecil poised himself atop a rail and proceeded contrary to the direction of the train, as if walking into the past, with each tie representing a stitch in time.

For Baker, Cecil was far more than just one who clung to the band's endeavors with an equivalent vigor. He served as a touchstone to days gone by, sparking memories of Baker's younger years, memories that would never have surfaced if Cecil hadn't pushed him into moving out of a life in stalemate and doing something profound with his music.

Now five years later and two thousand miles away from Baker's roots, his past was becoming much clearer. And these historical thoughts were reoccurring with less regularity the farther he drifted away from the Keys, distinctly separating the former from the present. Heading west had taken him out of a scene that had gotten all too uneasy. Being shot had thrust him into the unfamiliar territory of victimhood. The beauty of the coastline, the storybook architecture, became lost on him. He began to notice a world tainted with greed and prejudice. Fear was a new palpable emotion that took hold during moments of baseless vulnerability. But both maturity and distance helped to pull him away from his post-traumatic anxiety. And like an inmate recalling jail time, he found the depiction was not as bleak now that he was free.

Baker and Cecil had known each other for years, though Baker could never pinpoint when his friend first came into his life. Whenever the precise day had been, it coincided with a newfound interest in renovating his constitution, which could not begin without a return to the steps of Holy Trinity, to, as Baker called it, "get right with the Man."

After his hand had recouped enough strength and feeling, Baker joined the church band for the Saturday youth mass. These were simple tunes from the church hymnal just to keep up his most standard chops, to lay the groundwork for goals that were now far more ambitious, for he wanted not only to return to his former abilities but to blow right by them. And a style he had never before considered was suddenly the very tactic that would propel him farther from the ordinary.

Once Baker determined his fret hand was ready to take more punishment, he founded a flamenco trio. Playing afternoons in the open-air bars on Duval, on the promenade of Mallory Square, was taxing as the scolding rays of the Southern sun caused waves of sweat to pour down his pumping forearms. But during each rapid passage, Baker's mind was out of body as he noticed striking improvements from days gone by, as he now picked the strings cleaner than ever, playing at the speed of sound in a whirlwind of succinct accuracy.

Baker enjoyed his newfound style despite missing out on the real money, earned when the sun went down and the "Parrotheads," the rockers, came to play. Baker had been a rocker all his life, but upon moving away from all he knew, he broadened his wits and skill through the study of such ancient Spanish lightning rhythms. The long afternoons of sitting on stools, crouched over his guitar, had given him the posture of a man twice his age. But these gigs, which left him sore and dripping wet, had cleansed his soul, rinsing his mind of the hazy do-nothing days spent playing glam rock for nothing more than shits and grins.

Baker heard what he thought was Stevie Wonder's "Fingertips." But it wasn't the rip-roarin' version. It had been cut down in half-time.

The rails came to a junction. It was raining so hard, he recalled, as hypnotic streetlights flashed by the ambulance windows, heading for surgery in Miami.

One bullet had gone clean through his side, the other through his left hand, breaking ligaments to pieces with what was estimated to be considerable tendon damage. But how vital this hand was to his future as a musician was all he mumbled before the general anesthesia took hold, hoping the surgeon might just concentrate a little harder, cut down on the small talk over his limp body.

"Okay, Mr. Faraday, I need you to count backward from one hundred."

"P-l-l-l-e-e-e-a-s-e."

"Mr. Faraday?"

"B-e-e-e care-ful . . ."

Hours later, Baker's eyes cracked open, to find a nurse leaning over him, sliding out the intravenous needle from the top of his hand. She saw by his quick snap to attention that he needed confirmation. "The surgeon deemed the operation a complete success," she said in a smile as white and clean as a sterile bedsheet.

A half-truth, as Baker would find out years later, as the accident had given life to a risk, a disclaimer that came from such a precise form of operation, for bones could be set blindfolded by the sure-handed doctor, but the plexus of his hand linked the speedway from the brain, and Baker's had been muddled with thorough exactness by the bullet, creating a detour that short-circuited his most significant sense of touch.

But the doctors couldn't bring themselves to dash the young man's dream. After all, future detriments were not a certainty. And certainty was what these practitioners stood behind, a wall that made them feel secure in their decision not to impart the harsh truth, of a future of pain and inflammation he would most likely have to endure, and an arthritic condition as a worst-case scenario. Yet there was a slim chance of full recovery, and this remote possibility was all that was required to serve up the catchall excuse for not going into too much detail. Next patient . . . please.

During the weeks Baker's hand was immobilized, he often found himself on the floor, doing something he hadn't done since he was eight years old. With hands together, slowly rocking, he prayed for enough strength to return. "If you can hear me, God, I . . . I could use a little help here."

Baker knew not what to say, feeling somewhat embarrassed despite making his case in private. It began as no more than a plea out of fear and desperation. A proud young man was Faraday, but the harassing thoughts of losing everything he held dear haunted him. Fear threw him into shifting human themes from what was a perceived order of things to the genuine disorder of his reality. His friends were there; they were advocates and beautiful smoke blowers of the bright side. But it was his impromptu conversations with the Lord, now reaching an almost meditative state that took the jungle rot of pessimism away.

Baker did not form his bond out of thin air. Still, somehow, at some point, the air began to fill with His presence. *Why was I shot here?* Baker asked God as he pointed to his bandage. *And here?* He continued, looking up, touching his side.

As Baker moved farther down the tracks, he thought of one poignant moment, the one aspect of that night in Key West that overshadowed even the blinding pain of the bullets. Remaining at the forefront of the mystery was the stranger. Through his tearing eyes, he had caught a glimpse of a man. *Was I carried to the curb?* The feeling of floating was first discounted as the state of his condition. His hair was stroked with kindness. Then the words, whispered gently, just in front of the blare of distant sirens, *do not deny the vicissitudes, Baker Faraday. This begins a succession of events. Be prayerful . . . to see the light. Pray for me.* That single intimate moment could not be denied. When the storm cleared and the hibiscus opened to the light of the moon, the groveling thoughts of an agnostic man would begin to align, marking a way back to the path toward righteousness.

From that moment, his transcendental choice to follow Christ was felt like rip currents against his body, pulling Baker Faraday away from a mindset of haughty infallibility. He had spent most of his young life resolved to be evermore unhappy, blaming anyone but himself for his failures. But over time, such a stance began to seem pathetic, not a stance at all. He came to realize he had spent his life leaning on one crutch, then another, poised as a series of unfounded philosophies that Baker never bothered to validate. In contrast, Baker bore witness to something profound that stormy night. And that was more tangible than anything he had taken to be truth.

The rails approached a tunnel, the darkness formless and menacing as to cause Baker to stop in intimidation. He stood motionless in front of the passage, realizing he had far removed himself from tangible reality. He desired to go on. The memories were there, waiting for him. But Baker became more concerned with oncoming trains, of ending up like Wile E. Coyote, stuck to the face of the speeding engine.

Baker heard a nearly inaudible chuckle from the opposing rail, but when he smiled in Cecil's direction, no one was there.

"He never *is* too big on goodbyes," he said into the ominous tunnel, which returned his echo. Taking one last deep breath, he leapt onto the other rail to make his way back up the spine of Father Time, back to the present, and his band.

Baker saw Murphy sitting outside the motel room, staring skyward, tipping a bottle of SoBe, the green-tea flavor, to his lips. He flanked him on the step, and the two soaked in the night, sharing in a quiet guilt for not getting out to the mountains more often.

"How was your sound?" asked Murphy.

"Great," answered Baker, not relinquishing his gaze into the sky.

It was a question Murphy put forth after every performance. He hadn't joined the group on qualifications. Murphy had simply been Baker's coworker in carpentry and close friend. In spending long days with Baker, hearing him go on and on about his new band, the one that would be called "Alive and Well," with such regularity, Murphy formed a theoretical bond with men he had yet to meet. And when he was ultimately asked to participate in their quest, Murphy, being a devout Christian for as long as memory served, was more than willing to take on the responsibility: captain the band's sound, and give insightful feedback whenever necessary.

Not a skilled sound technician by any means, Murphy broke down the board in offbeat terms so as to diminish its daunting presence. The thirty-two channels of bus levers were his "Beam me up, Scotties"; the multicolored cables of auxiliary sends and returns were "the arteries," the digital display "Mother." After figuring in the assortment of doohickies and thingamabobs still waiting for Murphy-speak nomenclature, Baker began shunning his own technical interpretations, now referring to getting the right stage mix as "finding the happy place."

Every gig was a learning experience, but as Baker had predicted, he excelled, improving more each night. For Murphy Lafollette was a problem solver. He owned a peculiar intellect that reeled under hair that seemed to be on its own agenda, forever unkempt, as if searching for a legitimate style. From behind thick lenses that optically distorted his green eyes, Murphy steered the band not only in technical terms but as the house shrink as well.

A nerd through his formative years, Murphy had been the subject of many schoolyard torments. During situations that were sure to end with an ice pack on the eye or underwear hiked up his backside, he found a way to overcome such inauspicious moments. Rather than allow an emotional scar to open, his faith helped him gain a moral dominance over the aggressor. By not cooperating in the ignorance of the moment, he won every time. And this confidence lent Murphy the ability to feel altogether comfortable in his own skin, which is why he remained a nerd to this day.

Finding the way to beat fear allowed Murphy to profess on the basis of it, asserting anxiety as the underpinning for most cold-footed apprehension, the manifested butterfly that fed on trepidation like a tapeworm. As the subject of so much juvenile harassment, a man looking up from five and a half feet could see almost any of life's problems as a bully personified. And to Murphy, bullies were never smarter than he was.

Yet reveling in the perspective of a wonk had its drawbacks. There was one of life's variables that left him utterly perplexed. He could take on almost any harsh situation thrown his way. But women were not so hostile; therefore, to Murphy, they were unreadable, a Kryptonite against all rationale. Among those who knew him best, his shyness toward the opposite sex was legendary.

Minutes passed before Baker broke the silence. "If your band rips, I mean, really finds a way to ascend to the spiritual plane, but there is no one there to embrace it, how much sound does it really make, Murph?" He rose to pace out his thoughts. "The place was crowded tonight, but it was a saloon, full of altered states. The only time we don't get harassed for professing our faith is playing underground at Christian clubs or in bars, like tonight, where so many patrons are too out of it to notice. Then what good is it?"

Murphy sat quietly, closing his eyes to think a moment. "You are Alive and Well," he said finally, "the unwavering performers for the Almighty. You've created a sound rarely heard before. But ability is ignored when Christianity is seen as some kind of offense to the masses." He took a slug of his tea. "Manly Hall once wrote, they are the invisible powers behind the thrones of earth, and men are but marionettes, dancing while the invisible ones pull the strings."

"And the marionettes are the nonbelievers?" asked Baker.

Murphy shrugged. "It's very easy to be agnostic, or atheist, or an overall pessimist for that matter. Having faith takes a commitment, a giving of oneself. When it comes right down to it, living as an optimist can be a real pain in the ass. But to complain, to vent, is the quick and painless tonic that releases the pressure. It takes no effort to be negative because there is no willingness to resist it. So the weakest are willing to get pulled around."

"It's like the old saying," added Baker. "If you stand for nothing, you fall for anything."

"I believe so."

Baker crossed his arms in reflection. "I was once agnostic." He was still pacing, moving stones around with his shoes. "It's one thing to be skeptical but a whole other thing to reach the point of hating every aspect of God. How can anyone be so offended to the point of lashing out?"

"They do like to pick a fight," answered Murphy, "but people of real faith have found stillness in varying degrees, which leads to a contentment that inhibits our ability to retaliate. To fully love God is to cancel all accounts of cynicism. This is what we work toward. However unattainable it may be, it is our chosen path. Meanwhile, slowly, methodically, our messengers get picked off along the way."

"Hmmm. Destroy the messenger and you destroy the message."

"Yup, and we present ourselves as the easiest of targets."

"As Christ did."

"That's right."

A few seconds passed and Murphy felt the tension winding around their conversation. "What, Baker?" he mocked. "You getting cold feet? Should we come with a disclaimer on our playbills? We could change over to some derivative of pop rock."

"Hmph. No way, my friend," chuckled Baker. "It's the persecution that emboldens me."

The two rose up off the stair to make their way back to their room, when Baker slowed his soundman's step.

"Appreciate you coming way out here, Murph. I mean, as usual, we couldn't have done it without you."

Murphy scoffed at Baker's gratitude. "Are you kidding?" He wafted his arms about. "Here in the mountains . . . listening to such an astute version of rock 'n' roll? This *is* church, my friend."

"Don't you mean a devout form of rock 'n' roll slash funk mix with jazzy overtones and an occasional rap?"

"Yeah, Baker. You got it. But can you explain it in two words?"

Baker stopped for a moment, putting his hands deep into his pockets. "Ya know, Murph, no. No, I can't."

Murphy's voice trailed off as he left Baker alone in thought. "Simplicity calls for refinement. Sometimes less is more. Revel in each accomplishment my friend, it's the manna along the path to your ultimate destination."

Moby, the bass player of Alive and Well, mixed another drink, anxiously awaiting Baker's return. Dolf patted his pockets in an ill-fated attempt to locate his American Spirits. "Ay, Mobe, I gotta feed the monkey. Lemme bum one o' those cigs off you."

Moby languidly stretched across the counter, his back cracking like splintering wood as he reached to grab his Marlboros. He carefully tapped out a smoke, tossing it end over end to his drummer. Dolf reached up to catch the cigarette but missed, the filter end ricocheting off his forehead.

"Nice catch, bruh. Good thing I didn't send the lighter."

Moby returned to looking toward the door, willing it to open. To redirect his restless mind, he pulled on a few greasy strands of his pyrotechnic-red hair, which looked startlingly so much aflame under the fluorescent kitchen light. He tugged to the point of dull pain, but nothing could slow his pressing need for feedback on the evening. Ultimately, he lofted his usual question into midair, directing it at no one in particular. "So . . . what d'ya think?"

Dolf doggedly thrummed his pockets, on a hunt for something to fire up his smoke. "About what, our play or the digs?"

"There were some people coppin' a serious buzz by the end of the night," said Nat. His head sounded in echo from the refrigerator as he foraged for something to fill the void in his stomach. "Man, you see people when they drunk way too much? They be talkin' to ya, but they eyes be missin' yours, busy lookin' off over your ear or somethin', I mean, motor skills completely shot. With that kinda focus, how they gonna find their casa. I know they ain't no cabs up here. Might be uh, uh, horse-drawn wagon or somethin'."

"Toro, toro, taxi," answered Dolf out of the side of his mouth, clamping down on his still-unlit smoke.

Moby stretched his memory. "I got it! Mark Knopfler . . . Dire Straits . . . 1980. Loved that song."

"You can still love it, Mobe," said Nat. "Songs don't die." Standing aside Moby, Nat put his arm around him and sang a chorus.

*No fears alone at night she's sailing
through the crowd
In her ears the phones are tight and the music's
playing loud.*

It was a consenting sentiment of the group that Nat was the consummate front man for Alive and Well, rating high marks in all the meaningful aspects of portraying the social device onstage. He had an uncanny knack for figuring the mood of a room. Nat owned the intrinsic ability to find a common ground with the crowd that linked the audio to the visual. Whether he came off morally philosophic, sinfully erotic, or rashly rebellious, Nat always carried the confidence and honesty of unmixed intentions.

He was an exceptionally good-looking black man, wiry strong, with a bone structure that crafted his face to perfection, leaving no aspect rounded, incomplete. His eyes were large, deep, and kind. His cheeks were profoundly defined, with lips that were Creole thin, breaking often into smiling beams of bigheartedness that one could not help but contagiously absorb. Nat shaved his head close, exposing a few veins, which protruded like meandering rivers from his temple and neck, connecting his potent appearance to a naturally composed physique that looked chiseled from stone.

He had witnessed too many candy-coated Christian groups, led by a nasally voiced front man with limited moves. Nat would have none of it. He traveled the room, belting forth impassioned lyrics written most often by his hand. And this knack for soul and twisted wordplay fit together with a sound that bounded forward, at full steam. It was a style that maintained their enthusiasm. To play any different was to smother in mediocrity. Their sound was experimental, which made it distinctive, using the harder edge of rock and funk to cast a dissenting vote against the social and musical status quo. It was more cerebral with a vein of avant-garde dissonance.

Alive and Well saw their style as what set them apart. But it was soon found to be an imposing dilemma. They didn't quite fit into any radio-station format, Christian or otherwise. They couldn't be conveniently pigeonholed in the record store under the universal categories of rock and pop. They just slipped through the cracks, unable to achieve a mass appeal, leaving them underexposed and, too often, virtually alone with their sound.

Baker shivered at the thought of where they would be without Nat. In him, he had found the quintessential voice to spread God's word. And his bighearted nature was definitely a plus in a band that, on their own social accounts, weren't out to win any employee-of-the-month awards.

Dolf unlaced his Chuck Taylor high-tops, his shoes of choice for efficient feel on his kick bass. "Anyway, I liked the scene for the most part. I felt the crowd, bein' mostly townies and all, were kind of bona fide in a way. No bullshit about 'em." He continued to tap each shirt pocket several times for his lighter. "I really was dead certain we'd be playin' for a bunch'a stoics, like cigar-store Indians, up here, ya know?"

For the purpose of taking out a pesky fly, Dolf took a *Guitar Player* magazine from the coffee table and rolled it into a tight baton. In taking a vigorous swat, he wobbled a lamp. The fly avoided its aggressor's wild swing, landing lightly onto Dolf's blond, Billy Idol–spiked hair, rubbing its legs together and laughing its laugh in a pitch only a dog could hear.

"And they do take their drinkin' serious around here," said Dolf, continuing with the night's summation. "I had one belligerent ask me if he could play my set during break. What's up with that? Almost had to run 'im from the place myself."

"Afraid that booze hound might give you some pointers?" said Moby, taunting.

Dolf pointed a wary finger in Moby's direction. "Don't start." He flipped open a book of motel matches, to find none inside. "But to answer how I think we did, it's my opinion that we rocked the house, small house that it is."

Behind his Tribes, Dolf kept a heavy-duty beat for Alive and Well. But his tendency to drink heavily during gigs was a growing problem, causing hiccups in the tempo, an irritating flaw that could stop the most cutting musical movement in its tracks. And such a weakness in his character was becoming burdensome for his band, who could only hope his slipups in cadence would remain few and far enough between as to avoid public scrutiny.

With an excess of alcohol in his system, rarely would Dolf become a clown. Rather, he defined the acrimonious pose of a bad drunk, often sinking into a blue funk, becoming edgy and irritated toward strangers and friends alike. With

Dolf's brain marinating in bourbon and rum, his perception of meaning would turn blurry. He would frequently blow a matter-of-fact statement into something biting, derogatory to his ear only. And when his down mood was amplified, whether by accident or by design, Dolf's fists were known to come up. His fighting had caused the band to be exiled from three venues in Denver, and he was himself persona non grata in several other drinking establishments about town.

As long as he was able to zone in on his instrument, Dolf remained pacified. It was moments of intense concentration that seemed to put him at ease. Murphy had figured that was Dolf's reasoning for picking up chess as a sideline, to keep his mind occupied, fully absorbed in the competition, the test of skill. These days, he was never without his travel board and sack of black and white pieces, begging within his burgeoning dependence for a game. And his friends could only accept the challenge in fear of the alternative, taking turns when the beckon arose, to be checkmated by the ever-improving master in no time at all.

It had been a slow digression, so slow that one who did not know him well would not see the symptoms, but it was a fact to Baker and the others that Dolf was losing bits of his former self with each day. Eventually, the group stopped trying to rationalize the arbitrary behavior, chalking it up as a terrible habit to be ignored whenever possible, only jumping in when he needed the sedative of their calming words. And upon dousing another ignited fuse, they lamented a predisposition he had never invited.

Dolf bore the markings of a schizophrenic, and dealing with large crowds was not his strong suit. His quiver full of addictions helped him to mask the effects such a mob had on his mind. Puffing on smokes, slugging coffee, or drowning in whiskey is what got him through each night. With the help of Murphy's insight, Baker realized the anxiety that created such a down state was more complex than a simple boozing debauchery, and he shared these thoughts with the other band members, hoping they might just be patient with him. Murphy's psychoanalytical theory was that he was predisposed to mental illness, an irrational behavior that lay hidden for years, becoming noticeable only months ago. It could be building, Murphy warned, pointing out the growing delusions, hallucinations, and roller coaster of emotions. After touching on the fact Dolf had yet to fully realize anything was wrong, they all felt remorse and worry for him, holding back to support rather than rag too much on his Jekyll and Hyde mood swings.

With regard to religion, Dolf was indifferent. He would simply play anything in order to play with Baker Faraday. And Baker loved Dolf unconditionally, flaws and all, and he would pray for his friend each day in a hope to get him to take the journey into the arms of God. It was a certainty in Baker's mind that the Holy Spirit would lead Dolf to understand his situation. Until then, it seemed little could be done.

Baker and Murphy reappeared, and Moby tossed Baker a bottle of water. Baker had given up alcohol shortly after his accident. Murphy had never touched the stuff. Moby chucked a bottle of beer a little harder at Jimmy the Mole, who had been virtually invisible since they returned from the bar, long gone, lost in the electric glow of late-night television. The evening's events had little effect on the keyboardist's concerns, and it pissed Moby off to no end.

Jimmy gripped his beer bottle but couldn't budge the cap. "Somebody get me an opener."

Dolf reached over and grabbed the bottle from Jimmy. And with his mammoth paws appearing to swallow the beer, he twisted the cap free with little exertion. "Damn, Mole, maybe ya need to get off the couch and get some exercise."

Jimmy sneered at Dolf's suggestion, contorting his expression to match his sallow Goth face. His head sank into his shoulders as if he was chilled to the bone, bloodless, climbing out of his own grave. "Yeah, whatever, now where's the remote control?"

"The last place you left it, bruh," ragged Moby.

Moby did a slow strut over to Baker, who was now sitting quietly in the corner. He rapped him on the back with his knuckles to see if anyone was home. "Baker, give us your synopsis, bro."

Baker slowly leaned back into a pea-green BarcaLounger. "A good night . . . I think."

Such a skimpy answer prompted Moby to delve further into the show, dissecting the performance into small bits of brilliance. He stirred his Early Times and Coke, his fingers going round and round, causing the required whirlpool effect. "You know, about that sound check tonight. Some of my all-time favorite moments are when we free jam like that. Nobody even knows it's not anything we've ever done before, especially when Natty's ad-libbin' like he does."

Nat was the subject of his drummer's beckoning for a chess match and sat waiting while Dolf held his chin in his hand, pondering over the rolled-out travel board, never removing his eyes from the game. "Yeah, but we need to figure out how to end it—Dolf's lookin' at me, I'm lookin' at Mobe, you're lookin' at Bake, and well, ya know, Bake's just got his eyes closed in rapture the whole time."

Moby turned again to Baker. But Baker looked lost within the confines of his mind, staring with passive allure at the fly camped on Dolf's head. He repeated the thought once more. "Yo, Bake, what did you think of those intros to the first and second sets when we just groove like that?"

Baker interlocked his fingers, bending them back and forth to cause enough discomfort to zone back into the moment. "I love those segments. They kinda define us, you know? It's like a warning—here it comes, people, a joyful noise unto the Lord." He tipped up his water. "As far as an ending . . . tomorrow, just follow me. I'll get us out."

Moby looked down into his glass. "Okay, good. Tomorrow, then."

Nobody bothered to include Jimmy. He just seemed too lost, transfixed on the glimmer of the screen, intrigued by the competition taking place on *American Gladiators*. The one lasting feature to Jimmy the Mole's lifelong lobotomy attributable to excessive television was his mastering of an assortment of movie lines long since committed to heart. He had sat through the original Star Wars trilogy at least twenty times. "No . . . try not . . . do . . . or do not. There is no try," he remarked in his best Yoda impersonation.

The five all suspended what they were doing to look at Jimmy with crinkled brow. "Wha?"

Following the brief tangent, Dolf proceeded to end the chess game with one fluent slide across the board, queen to bishop six.

They broke off one by one just before the predawn hour. Only Baker lay awake in the double bed he shared with Jimmy, hands interlocked behind his head, staring into a ceiling of textured drywall. Jimmy was sleeping hard, letting loose on a mousy wheeze that sounded like nothing Baker had ever heard before. But that wasn't what was stealing his sleep.

He looked at his hands, at the thick calluses he had developed with intention on his fingertips. He tracked the tight wrinkles in his palms caused by the dry Colorado air, the nicks and scrapes that, as a carpenter, come with the territory.

They look different in the moonlight, worn and old. Abused, he thought to himself as he clenched and released, watching the veins in each forearm rise to attention. *Or no, well used, like tools of the trade, yeah, machinelike, devices of the flesh.*

Still, he wondered of the toll this lifestyle would take on his aging body, about how long his hand could keep up with what he asked it to do time after time. When would that day come when he would awaken to the stiffness and not be able to make it go away?

He wondered about Moby, the eldest at thirty-two. How long would he last, given his growing disenchantment? Baker had seen the look in his eyes after a bad night, the strain of half-dead fatigue, second thoughts swimming around in his mind. In witness to his frustration, Baker could only sit with a tight lip, not wanting the true answer, not wanting to give his bassist an out, a reason to quit. Baker knew they could do without Moby's grumpy behavior, his untoward chicanery, but his bass play harmonized with his every idea and was an almost-irreplaceable facet, one that had taken precious time to build.

Nat was twenty-eight, but his age really meant nothing. With an inner spirit of boundless determination, able to magically project his highest aspects at all times, Nat was one that maintained a raw drive to match Baker's own. *Will Nat get tired of it all?* he pondered with trepidation. *The small stages, the empty houses, the tireless practices that might fail to feed his need for release. Will it leave him to dream about other plans that may not involve this band?* Baker knew a singer like Nat needed the occupation, the affairs with popularity, to keep his motor revving. Bands with more successful projects had approached him, those who had been awed by his method, in need of that advertisement onstage. Nat, however, would merely be flattered and send them on their way, giving Baker that look from across the room like everything was fine. "Why should the devil have all the good music?" he would say.

But Baker felt all the more culpable for not being able to provide the stimulus his front man needed with more regularity.

There was a gap of several years down to Dolf and Jimmy. They were not yet at such a point of feeling the toll of the long shows and late nights. Embodying the ambivalence of immaturity, they lived in secular carelessness, able to toy with the illusion of success as defined by an unclean heart. The others pushed them to strive for a greater sense of devotion, but they scoffed at the gesture. For now, it was all fun and games, and at the end of the day, Baker couldn't rebuke those he loved both as friends and as children who grope in the dark.

He couldn't help but deliberate the facts, wondering whether it was prudent or prodigal to allow these thoughts to weigh so heavily on his mind. Baker rose to look out the window, at the stars, thinking of the night's performance over again.

For Alive and Well, such positive occurrences happened every so often, on those special evenings when everything seemed to gel. The astrologer may say it's when the night sky comes into alignment, but it struck Baker that it took little insight to know these things, for celestial patterns run in the predictable scientific manner of intelligent design. This aspect bared only subtle exception to what was already anticipated. To a musician, it was when everyone clicked to the same notions, both the entertainer and the entertained. And those lucky enough to stumble upon such a desired episode feasted that much more on their exhilaration.

He desired one simple hardheaded want, to do what he loved full time. And in order to do this, Baker Faraday had to take the road less traveled. Gripped in the throes of Christian faith, he found amplifying God's word was the only way. The choice had proved to be long and arduous, but to Baker, nothing gained with ease could be appreciated with equal vigor. A guitar player of such extraordinary skill could find success on ability alone, but Baker required penitence to find enlightenment. And sometimes the contrition felt as if it would overcome his will. But to pick up and play his Takamine, his Fender Strat, took every sting out of living such a hard life, almost always.

A life full of thought and purpose was the only way to rise up and prevail over whatever feasted on humanity. Baker knew the only way to reach his audience was to transcend where so many now held their values, which to Baker no longer lay in a heart sealed behind seven pair of tough, true ribs. Rather, for so many, it had been enticed out to sit just behind a layer of thin skin, weak and impressionable, poised to adopt each and every subordinate standard of someone else seen daily on television.

For Alive and Well, results were coming slowly, based not on lack of effort or talent but on what the public deemed important, interesting, and hip. And it was this ever-so-consequential aspect that stepped on his band's hopes so often, leaving them flat on the ground, to slowly get up, brush off, and try again.

The rear window framed the high plains, the western mountain range in the distant background. The first light of morning was creeping skyward. *Gotta get some sleep*, he thought. Under Baker's nose, along the windowsill, was his tiny pharmacy of vitamin supplements, Tolectin and Demerol. He bent down to look through the opaque-orange pill bottle that held tens of little white knockouts. Baker squeezed the bottle tight in his hand, weakly willing the pain to emanate enough and give him good reason to shake out three or four tablets.

The discomfort became noticeable; it started to burn but held to the point of still being tolerable.

At the cliff's edge of his mind, there was nothing, no bottom. To an addict, it meant that there was no perceptible consequence to prevent the indulgence. Yet this pitch-black pit was still daunting to Baker. With what remained of his strength, he deliberately raised his head from the darkness and up into the light. As he breathed in His presence, Baker prayed slowly, softly. And the pain began to subside, just enough.

Not tonight. Baker gently set the prescription back on the sill, wiping his hand across his shirt as if the tug of need still clung to his skin. Putting his hands on his head, Baker breathed deeply, when a glimmer caught the corner of his eye. Across the room, his Takamine stood against an old rustic dresser. The moonbeams danced off the nickel and silver frets, as if beckoning Baker for a quick play. Grinning at what seemed such a personified invitation, Baker walked over to the guitar, flexed his fingers, and pulled the neck from its lean.

Sleep could wait a little longer.

2

UNSEALED DEALS

Moby stepped into the bathroom. Launching into a fit of hacks and coughs, he lifted the toilet lid to spit. But he didn't spit; rather, he let the mucus hang and drop into the bowl, causing the water to plunk as if a quarter had been released from eye level.

"Nasty, Mobe," said Nat, screwing up his face, put off by such a rude hawking burst. "Close the door 'fore you get us all ill."

"Sorry, bruh. I'm feeling a little phlegmbouyant this evening."

Feeling the surprise onrush of intestinal pressure, Moby shut the bathroom door, dropping his black Levi's quickly in answer to his body's opinion of the diet he'd been keeping. Fifteen minutes and a half roll of toilet paper later, he flipped on the bathroom fan and exited with a strange smirk of pride.

He stopped only briefly to announce the invisible danger lurking beyond the door. "DO NOT go in there!"

To the disgust of his band, the odor followed Moby from the bathroom, triggering everyone's gag reflex in tandem. A wilt of remorse briefly ran across Moby's face. But ultimately, he resolved to merely chuckle at his own brief outcry of inner sympathy.

Moby was prone to behave like a pig. But the fault could not lie entirely on the simple mind of one who grew up in the Bronx. He was raised by an aunt and uncle, but more often, St. Xavier Catholic Church and Father Leo, whom he came to see whenever the punishments at home exceeded his considerable toughness.

He had missed out on the part of childhood where manners were learned, when deviating from the rule meant a grounding or withheld allowance. In *his* upbringing, delinquency meant the belt from Uncle Frank, a method severely lacking in constructive criticism, leaving only the sharp conclusion, the result of the defining warning, "Don't do that or else."

This one-sided rearing of a boy through his adolescence left even the most obvious aspects of societal protocol lost amid the anger of a child who knew only forceful retaliation, leaving any sprouts of chance civility to decompose into what could have been. But Moby was not one to look for pity from a slighted nurturing. He was proud of his hard-boiled inheritance and wouldn't have traded his childhood with anyone. To live wild had the advantages of running with the moon whenever he pleased, to loiter with the older streetwise swindlers, learning the ropes between the red-brick walls of alleyways and the concrete-block confines of holding cells.

Having to rely on self-survival was a challenge he grew to relish. It was a fact that kept goodwill deep inside, relegating itself only to show its essence to those with an earned confidence, for Moby respected only those people who were deemed in his book as having their shit together, the ones able to supply the required basis, the standard that held up against the two strikes Moby attached to every first impression. But once Baker cajoled him away from Fistfight, an ashtray gig group getting by on Aerosmith and Bad Company covers, Moby quickly took his new friend into his trust. And once Baker smoothed over the brunt of Moby's most callous tendencies, the others found a camaraderie that was rock solid, bonding the group together with the consistency of well-mixed cement. His friends could let his shameless crudity, his overt brazenness, slide, knowing he would forever be rough around the edges but certain that he bled true blue.

The odor waned, allowing everyone to collect themselves. They gathered in a circle in the middle of the apartment. "You wiped, right?" asked Jimmy before taking Moby's hand in prayer.

"Mmmm, I think so, bruh," answered Moby.

Each member of Alive and Well bowed his head. Even Dolf and Jimmy looked to the floor, out of respect for their leader, who began:

Holy Lord, You are the master of all creative things, including the gift of music. Be with us as we celebrate Your gift, as we play and sing with each other, as we raise our voices and our instruments to Your glory. We ask for this presence in the name of Your son, Jesus Christ, who lives and reigns with You now and forever. Amen.

The band began gathering the required necessities lying about before taking to the night's celebration. In forecast of the swelling, Baker downed a Tolectin. Moby grabbed his chrome-brushed lighter, his smokes. Nat shook out one mint Tic Tac. Jimmy checked his ears, making sure his piercings were all tight. And Dolf took the coffee pot to his travel mug.

After Dolf spent a moment zoning in on his target, his pour missed its mark and formed a pool around the mug's base. Slowly creeping its way to the edge of the shellacked wooden table, it began filling in the natural imperfections of knots and wormholes in the wooden floor at Dolf's feet.

"You shouldn't even be drinking that, bruh," Moby advised. "You're already wound tighter than your snare head."

Dolf finished pouring, ignoring any cream or sugar, those ingredients that took the bitter oomph out of his liquid adrenaline. "I have to have it. What can I say? I'm an addict, the end result of working two hostile jobs. I need the boost, know what I'm sayin'? You're talkin' to a log skinner by day and a drummer by night, for crap's sake. And my snare is tuned fine, thanks very much, Mobe."

The subject suddenly perked Baker's attention. He had been waiting weeks to bring up Dolf's snare and saw his opportunity cracking open. "Actually, Dolf, about your snare—did you ever think about tuning it different or maybe even getting another, something with a little throatier sound? Yours kinda comes off like a jazz snare, and with the force you use in hitting it, it makes for a hostile pitch sometimes. I don't know if it's meant for what we're trying to do."

Dolf held a well-inflated opinion of his playing and equated power and aggression as the all-important corner-stones of rock percussion. His chops were meaty, his snare crack crisp, every evening presenting another endurance test for his set. Now and then, the crash cymbal might fly off its stand. The shells of his maroon maple toms displayed inden-tations where brackets had been knocked loose.

Normally, he jumped all over anyone remarking nega-tively on his style or competence. But Baker was the undis-puted leader. Whenever he opened his mouth to give a little advice, it was justifiable and meant for the good of the group. This fact left Dolf to sit cringing into his black pool of caf-feine, with heat rising from his head, psychically visible to Baker, who bit down in regret for throwing a lit match into such a combustible area.

The perceived acrimony was palpable. Even so, Dolf knew he couldn't rebut Baker's view, for he always spoke with well-thought kindness, without the intention of ever lambasting anyone. When it came to the band, they all knew Baker's purpose was not to put down but to present a virtuous turn toward whoever went under his observation. Still, whatever good intentions were designed, the pill was always bigger for Dolf, unable to be swallowed easily but rather chewed on for a time before digesting what was truly benign medicine.

Becoming ever more leery of Dolf's temperament, Baker allowed the discussion to dissolve. To bring up more than one foible at a time would only further stoke the fires of his animosity, ruining the first point under a morass of defensive posturing. Next time, Baker would push further to nudge his drummer away from the standard two-and-four regiment, or hopefully reinforce the need to position his high-hat farther away, incorporating better feel, less strength. Privately, Baker planned rather than risk embarrassment for his friend. Next time, it would be a quiet one-on-one affair, discretion being the best tool, one in which Baker did his best work.

The front window rattled with a heavy-fisted knock, shaking the room from the prickly discussion.

"What the . . ." said Jimmy with a spasm of fright in his voice.

Baker glanced over to notice a disheveled sort cupping his hands against the panes and smiled at the sight of Cecil. He summoned to Baker to come outside. And Baker feigned a head nod to his friend and watched as he backed away, fading into the night.

"I'll see you guys at the bar," said Baker, removing himself without further explanation. His band just nodded and mumbled, accustomed to the impromptu tangents Baker was known to take, a trait simply referred to as "doing what Baker does."

After passing the Crazy River, Baker strolled past several storefronts to a snowmobile rental shop closed for the season. There, he found Cecil sitting on the wood planking, leaning back on a hitching post, a remnant built to resupply a bit of Western history. He was gently picking a soft melody on an ancient nicked-up Martin D-28. Baker instantly recognized Cecil was playing Cohen's "Hallelujah."

Baker leaned heavily into the hitching post. Panning the town, he allowed his mind to wander amid the heavenly sounds created by his friend's hand.

A surly figure materialized in the middle of the wind-swept street. His eye was patched and leaked a wicked white scar out the bottom. His long-rider was pulled back, exposing the glint on his pistol. The outlaw had his hands to his sides, twitching in anticipation of a duel. But Baker was quick with his thumb and index finger, taking a concise shot at his "Most Wanted" illusion, smiling with content as he fell to the ground in a heap of flesh and leather.

> *Maybe there's a God above,*
> *But all I've ever learned from love*
> *Was how to shoot somebody who outdrew ya.*

The raw undertones of an old acoustic pushed Baker into evoking his solo days, when he saddled the stool on open-mic nights.

He needed to break into the Denver music scene, so it seemed like a good idea at the time. But there were aspects of amateur night that felt like punishment to a man of Baker's ability. To sign up late was to play later, held captive by the sleepy-time theater of second-rate folk music, sitting for hours as one proletarian after another tripped through their strings, singing poetic reflections about botched relationships, long car drives, or man's best friend.

But when his turn ultimately arose, nothing could be played off key. To Baker, performing this way was an injustice to his guitar. His Takamine was treated with respect, like a lifelong partner he had grown so dependent on. And when he brought the guitar to life, the room, in a pleasant candlelight dim, fell silent. The left hand held the rhythm against the finger board as the right picked the strings cleanly, splitting the guitar into a harmonious duet of sound. The astounded crowd was composed almost entirely of aspiring musicians, who all waited impatiently to perform. But the next in line might not be so eager, wishing he wasn't following Baker Faraday.

He thought it would be a good place to find connections, but most of what he encountered were fellow guitar players struck by his way with the instrument. With Baker, things were unconventional, novel. His Takamine acoustic and his Fender Strat were his emotional bookends, lifelong therapies against whatever ailed him. Not playing was to regress into a wanton state of need, and this noticeable difference showed in the other performer's approach to their strings. Some had passion, but for many, their instrument merely served as filler, relying entirely on the words, singing the song, telling the story.

Some acquaintances from these open-mic sessions became students, serving as the income that kept him going toward his definitive pursuit. But to Baker's mounting disappointment, no one stepped forward with a deeper desire to find that spiritual bond. No. Rather, in cruel contrast to Baker's insatiable artistic appetite, they were satisfied with owning the minimum means, to play any Clapton or Dillon tune well enough to impress a handful of people at an impromptu gathering, perhaps a cute impressionable girl primed for the trickery of one who might know "Little Wing" but little else.

As time went on, Baker could no longer maintain enthusiasm for the passive sound of the acoustic. So light in his hands, his Takamine began to feel overplayed and tired. Amid the somber ambiance of amateur night, he could only fidget on the stool and force a smile when applause came his way. As he longed for a greater sound, missing the pop of the amp as he plugged into his solid-maple Stratocaster, banging out heart-pounding arpeggios or a hard-edged distortion that could vibrate a glass of beer off the edge of a table.

It had taken some time to acclimate to the cold. Even in the dead of summer, the Rocky Mountains can conjure a chill in the air. And it was such a sensation that brought Baker back, realizing Cecil was still playing, never interrupting but giving Baker's mind the room to run.

Baker returned to absorb the fortuitous tranquility with Cecil, as his friend always knew how to clear his mind before a show, putting him in the right state to perform.

It was a relationship precisely based upon a situation of peace between two people, Baker thought, as he turned back to the dusty street. The simplicity of his company breached upon being a prohibited act in today's subplot society, which was why, to Baker, Cecil was so righteous. He was a throwback to bygone days, becoming the ultimate contrast to the newly written mannerisms of techno-humanity. He was the principled id in the land of superegos, which was why he owned his life in a time when others were leasing theirs on someone else's terms.

Perhaps it was that Cecil felt invested in Baker's success, for he had offered Baker his wings, enough gumption to leave everything he had known. It was a difficult quest to handle alone. But Cecil was compelled to help bring six young men together, a supporting cast with enough qualities, quirks, and shortcomings that, if nothing else, would keep things interesting.

Baker felt a bump into his shoulder. Cecil pointed to his wrist and then to the saloon. He gave Cecil a light punch to the arm, pushing away in the direction of the stage, playfully whistling "Rocky Raccoon."

On the normal nights, the evenings when day-end darkness enveloped the well-known Denver streets of Broadway or Larimer, Alive and Well could get a pretty good idea of who would be coming out to see the show. They had no problem at set's end dispersing among the crowd to visit with both the young, enthusiastic Christians and the derisive patrons who wanted no part of the Lord on Saturday night. But for this one weekend, the comforting frequency of the usual was miles away.

During the summer, when Bear failed to find an interesting sound to put in the corner of his saloon, there was little excitement. Regulars deviated from the music with small talk, a drunken faraway look that only returned to focus at the end of a song, when a clap or two might sound from someone with the wherewithal to notice. But for two nights in mid-June, a time when Bear's schedule usually brought only lukewarm talent at best, Alive and Well provided a much-appreciated release against the boredom and idleness of a do-nothing town.

Word of mouth must have carried throughout the day, as Baker measured a larger attendance than the night before. And such a turnout was not lost on his band. Baker, Nat, and Murphy, the most devout members of Alive and Well, felt like Rocky Mountain missionaries, supplying a new sound behind an old ideal, pushing blood flow back into the hearts and minds of those who had gumption enough to rise from their seats and move to the beat.

The Crazy River was a sad excuse for a singles bar, though the regulars stopped giving a care long ago. Over the years, Fraser locals couldn't help but become casual acquaintances within such a small setting, and in gathering more and more information, they grew painfully familiar with one another. Ergo, pickup lines only fell from the mouths of the eager tourists, strangers out to get lucky in a strange town. With the men of Fraser, conversations were for the most part unceremonious. No inflated public accounts of oneself were ever practiced in the mirror while slapping on the cologne of choice. Such haughty exchanges were just not something anyone put in the forefront of their mind, and it was for this reason that conversation, when it occurred, came off refreshingly frank and sincere. It was the combination of booze and blissful ignorance that put everything on the level, where no one cared to look deeper into anything said, for it was figured nothing was to be found there. Where an overfocused swinger might manufacture evidence to put in place of an empty underlying meaning, the men and women of Fraser never went looking for it, feeling it was just not worth the energy to dig. And on an evening such as this, conversations were dropped for what was presented onstage.

> *The final verse of your curse brings a nourishing hope to us all.*
> *In the end, life begins; it's sad to watch you crawl.*
> *Must admit you had time to quit,*
> *But for you, it's a lesson hard learned,*

> *You done to taking and heart breaking; now*
> *you're getting burned.*
> *I hope you've learned,*
> *By He more gracious than yourself, you've been*
> *given a second chance.*
> *Protect your health, take the gift, and*
> *redeem yourself.*

"We'll be back for our last set in about fifteen," Nat assured through the mic, adding in a playful exaggeration, "and don't think you're leavin' now cause, uh, you'll miss the raffle for a week of free drinks. Ain't that right, Bear?"

The old barkeep looked up at Nat from under his lure-laden fishing hat, shaking his head and cracking a wide grin, happy to be pulling the tap for yet another pour.

People stood shoulder to shoulder at the bar, but as Baker approached, those camped out for most of the night parted the way, offering Baker a seat with kind but hackneyed words like "You rock, brother!" and "Awesome licks, man!" The proficient bartender that Bear was, he slid Baker a glass of iced tea, already known to be "the usual."

Baker took the beverage in the left hand, allowing the chill of the glass to soothe his arthritis, drop the swelling. He turned his back on the crowd, closing his eyes to enjoy the remedial therapy to his pain.

Moby came over to stand beside Baker. Realizing he was struggling, he put an arm around his friend, pulling him close. When it came to Baker's hand, it was a well-ingrained rule that nothing be said. His friends knew not to look at it, much less talk about it. Baker was wary to keep his pain hidden as best he could, but it was always a vain attempt to bury what loomed so large. He turned slightly, smiling at his friend's shot of encouragement.

"That's a new way to enjoy a drink."

Baker rotated away from Moby to the voice, realizing he must have been sitting there stoically gripping his glass for several minutes. A young woman was in the seat next to him.

"Kimberly," she said, holding up her glass of soda. Baker couldn't believe he had been couched so long without noticing such a stunning woman. *Damn, Baker, stop drifting off. Manage it. Manage it.* His gaze locked onto her brilliant eyes, like arctic sapphirres, allowing every allure to pull his attention away from the ache.

She was stylish for mountain life. Her body was fit but conservatively concealed under a thinly braided summer sweater, the color of eggnog, that hung low over her black leggings and nearly concealed her hands.

"I couldn't help but notice your, uh, guitar playing up there . . . not bad." She smirked sarcastically. "I take it you're the leader of this operation."

"Sometimes, Kimberly." He glanced back at Moby, who was mocking his bandmate by taking exaggerated passionate tokes on his unlit cigarette. "When it's needed."

"Well, for what it's worth, I'm impressed. The music is so, um . . ."

"Unexpected," Baker answered for her, anticipating she might need an explanation.

"Well yeah, but not by its skill but by its purity . . . artistically and, well, spiritually speaking. I mean, being a rock musician can be such a sordid occupation."

Baker looked to Bear, raising his glass for another, and one for the lady. "In this business, everyone's a dreamer. But if thoughts are corrupt, if they're not linked to a higher purpose, what's really been accomplished?"

Kimberly perked to the reply, the way he involved her in his answer by returning a question. "You mean the ends should justify the means?"

Baker was baffled yet stimulated that someone would want to delve further into the subject. He turned briefly to Moby, who gave a half smile, a nod to continue. "To desire is to obtain. To aspire is to achieve," he answered.

Kimberly pulled on the scrunchie that held her dirty-blonde hair in a manageable ponytail, releasing it to fall over each shoulder. "I concur. I mean, a person pushed around by outside conditions is doomed to fail." She gathered the lengthy dense locks up into her hands and scratched her scalp ferociously, unbinding the clumps, leaving a subtle crimp in the strands. Down it came again. "I bet you have a morass of negativity pushing on you for playing this music."

Baker was taken aback by the all-out sexiness of Kimberly's maneuver, causing a hiccup in his thought process. He shook his head and cleared his throat. "I guess it's not for everyone. But it's for me."

Murphy arrived at the bar but stalled a moment, plotting a way to cross between the conversation to pick up his lemon water.

"Uh, excuse me," he said, looking in Kimberly's direction, eyes darting to the ground. Frozen, he began to shift his weight from one foot to the other. Kimberly put a finger to his chin, lifting his head up to meet her gaze.

She was sensitive, knowing the dilemma her move just caused. "Lemon water, huh? Sounds good. Can I have a sip?"

"Well, I would but, uh, see, I don't know you and, uh . . ."

Kimberly nodded her head in understanding. "Germs, huh?"

Murphy fought to keep his head up, took a deep breath. "Bacteria, yes . . . millions . . . and . . . m-m-millions."

Baker broke in to rescue his friend. "Kimberly, this is Murphy, our soundman. Murph, Kimberly."

Murphy took another breath and exhaled. "Hi, Kimberly. It's nice a meet you."

"Pleasure," answered Kimberly, offering her hand.

To Murphy, saliva was impossible, the hand improbable. But she was pretty, with eyes so kind that it began to loosen the knot in his throat. He reached out and took her hand ever so gently. "I'm, uh, sorry about my drink, but, uh, there are things like streptococcus, gingivitis. There's even open sores that can—"

"O-o-o-o-kay, Murph," Baker interrupted. "Is there anything you need to do at the board before we start back up?"

"Yes," answered Murphy, almost too quickly. "There is something I, uh, need to do. Ex-cuse me." Murphy backpedaled a couple steps, banking off the crowd before disappearing behind those larger than him, which was nearly everyone.

"Umm, *your* name?" pressed Kimberly.

"Baker. Baker Faraday."

"Let me see *your* hand, Mr. Faraday," demanded Kimberly, in a flirting sort of way.

Baker reluctantly gave over his left hand. Kimberly took it gently, taking note aloud. "Rough and tough . . . high veins." She took Baker's hand to her nose. "No scent." She flipped it over. "And scarred, uh-huh, as a man's paw should be." She took a long draw from her Dr. Pepper. "For a guy like you, lofty ideals are a necessity, and scrapping to attain them builds your character. Doubt you speak much of literature, or interior design."

Baker rose to the examination. "Does the Good Book count?"

"Uh, no."

"Then your analysis is correct."

Kimberly paused to look at herself with Baker in the bar-back mirror. "I'll tell you what," she continued, "it's the damn narcissism in men these days, the self-conscious nature that feeds women's restlessness. Wish we had more like you out there."

Baker sat quietly, thinking of the longer hair he used to have, the oft-used question of what conditioner he used, and the disbelief when he said he never partook. "They say on television that men should get in touch with their feminine side," he recalled. "If everyone's feminine, I would think it would leave a lot to be desired, for a woman, I mean."

Kimberly pursed her lips, crossed her arms. "Ya know, you're right. Guys are such wussies these days. It's no wonder women are turning to women. Where are the Paul Newman, Clint Eastwood types?"

Baker saw the sudden troubled look of a young woman living their conversation. He could envision her last attractive boyfriend, for she could win any man, he thought. He felt compelled to reach out to take her hand but held up a moment before resting his back on the bar. "Have you ever tried church?"

Kimberly should not have been surprised by such a remark, but the mere mention sounded strange, so foreign, like something so freaking square as to never contemplate such a way of life. Still, as she looked at a man she quickly came to admire, such an option definitely had legs to stand on. "Will you be there?"

Baker leaned in close, close enough to penetrate the bubble of Kimberly's comfort zone. And Kimberly let him in, seeming secure in his company. "Every Sunday," he said, rising to return to the stage. "Every Sunday."

Nat was sitting at a table aside the stage and noticed Baker looking his way. And in reference to Baker's most recent encounter, he gave a sign of melodramatic approval, slowly drawing a bar napkin across his brow, dabbing away a sarcastic sweat of passion. Baker just shrugged his shoulders, hiding a content enjoyment that it was he, and not Nat, who just made time with the most beautiful woman in town.

Baker panned the crowd and found Jimmy pushing his way toward Murphy in earnest. The anticipated discussion over the sound mix was close at hand. He could only compress his lips, hoping Murphy spotted him in time.

It was like clockwork, as Jimmy always came by before a set. Murphy reached down to the board, nudging the keyboard levels up a notch just before he was close enough to see the layout. Unbeknownst to Jimmy, it had become the furtive rule between Murphy and Baker to bring down Jimmy's sound, equating his talents, or lack thereof, with how much his contribution needed to be heard.

The desire to succeed was on a different scale for Jimmy the Mole, embracing fame and fortune over the hardship it takes to get there. And in choosing this path, this conflict of interest, Jimmy could seldom allow himself to slip inside the music, to feel the ultimate movement and ride the same notion that the others shared so completely.

Without the will to master his instrument, Jimmy would turn to a certain musical chicanery, learning a few tricks to camouflage his play. He compensated for most of his inadequacies by hiding much of his performance behind the mantle of processed synthesizer washes, emulating a horn section or distorting his voice. Adding any frilly complexity with simplistic maneuvers soon became Jimmy's livelihood, the crutch that held him up onstage.

Piano, on the other hand, left less room for error and put him at the mercy of an observant crowd. When called upon to produce a more natural sound, he kept to neighboring keys, playing the whites with only one hand.

Baker had grown tired of these antics and was first to voice the idea of turning Jimmy down. He refused to feel remorse toward his viewpoint. It was simply an artistic price to pay for positioning the music to be less primary. Jimmy never noodled around on the keys by himself; rather, he left it idle until rehearsal, the moment when he *had* to play.

Baker looked to give Jimmy a bigger role, but nor could he sing, so backups were virtually dropped as well. Although he wore the headset each night with pride, thinking all the while his harmonies meshed well with Nat's voice, the electrifying front man would only act out a contrived symmetry with Jimmy, putting up with a voice that had no range. But neither Nat nor Baker could ever get to the point of mentioning anything. They loved Jimmy and pitied his insecurities. Anyway, Moby roasted him with enough big-brother tenacity to suffice for the lot of them.

Despite such shortcomings, everyone took an admirable credence toward Jimmy's hard work in setting up. He always volunteered to untangle the wreck of cords, tape them down, and plug them in. It privately was his way of truly contributing, knowing his musical abilities were a secondary aspect to his subsidy, even on such a basic but necessary level.

It was no secret that Jimmy's niche was entrenched in the fact that the majority of the equipment was his, as well as the space to practice. But more than the furnishings, the expense laid out just to be part of a band was the result of spending so much time in such close proximity with one another. It blended their souls, each becoming a piece of one another.

As part of their creed, Alive and Well would endeavor to see flaws as flaws of the whole. Bitching and moaning, voicing strong opinions, was part of the program, but the affection they held inside dampened anger in favor of acceptance for who Jimmy was, and what they all knew he could be.

At the very most, he looked the part of a rocker with an ironic perfection, in his long black hair and leathers, with jeans ripped fashionably at the knee. But behind the vanity of his pose, his friends only hoped he would stop settling for false comfort, hoping one day he would wake up with a new direction, a new outlook on music, on life. Though, for now, he would only provide the means and an occasional glimpse of intuitiveness onstage, proving to Baker and the others that Jimmy owned the required emotional spirit, it was only a matter of freeing it from the bondage of insecurity.

The band made their way back up onto the small stage, planking that was raised three inches off the barroom floor. All five managed to snugly fit upon it, with heels hanging off each side.

As soon as Baker had the guitar strap over his head, Moby started into a riff, speaking with his instrument a request to play "Friday's Gone." Baker and Moby were always on the same page onstage, and Baker nodded in agreement to his bass player's beckon.

Nat dropped the mic from his mouth for privacy. "They gettin' as weary as a spindly-legged bloodhound home from a day of trackin' a smelly shirt," he said, still having fun with the whole Western concept, noticeably feeling the effects of spending the weekend in a one-horse town.

"How about a buoyant melody with some heavy guitar statements?" answered Baker as he provided a steady intro.

> *Alone in the dark as I see you twist at sea,*
> *I'm hoping you'll come back to me.*
> *But it's all so clear in yesterday's arms, oh so near,*
> *The whispers in my sleep say…*

Even without a mic, Nat's voice had the power to punch the back wall. Spittle flew from his mouth as his chest, shining with sweat, heaved out the lyrics in masterful harmony. He was on, and the rest knew it. Moby retreated as far as possible to allow his singer a little more space, not ample distance but adequate to the point of Nat noticing and smiling in appreciation.

Alive and Well had performed as if it were their last-ditch attempt to get a foothold in this far-removed environment. Fraser could open things up, for down the road loomed the bigger tickets of Summit County, maybe even Vail or Aspen. A mountain tour this winter would be a blessing. Playing for hundreds rather than tens could provide a springboard to the next level. If that door could just open a crack, Baker was sure he could shoulder it the rest of the way no matter what pushed back on the other side.

The subsequent ovation was surprisingly healthy considering the hard-core patrons who remained. And after the final drunken expression of, "Don't quit. It's early. Ah, man," they began to disassemble their equipment.

Bear could have jumped over the bar in his excitement. Before they got too far into breaking down, the pleased owner approached to put a hand on Nat's back. "Don't worry about this tonight, fellas. You did really fine for me this weekend. Go on and enjoy your evening, what you have left of it."

Moby and Dolf snapped around to look at each other with eyes alight to the same notion. They made a beeline for the bar in an attempt to stretch last call, but Bear already had them lined up.

As the last dizzied patron was pointed homeward, Bear came quickly with the pay. "Well done once again, gentlemen. I haven't seen such an off-season crowd in a long while. Let's do it again sometime, okay?"

"Love to," said Baker, approaching Bear coolly, trying to hide his eager intent. "In fact, we have some free dates over the ski season?" An exaggeration, to be sure—Alive and Well's slate was basically clean.

"Well, uh, I'm booked through the winter, fellas."

Bear saw the look of dejection on their faces, a feeling that they had wasted their weekend. "Look, guys, lemme be straight. You have more talent than anyone I have seen in here since I opened the place twenty years ago." He raised his foot up on a chair, as if to give a life lesson to children sitting wide-eyed with legs crossed on the floor. "But now I'm going to tell you something I'm sure deep down you know. Christian music is a tough pill for folks. It makes them feel, well, uncomfortable. Your sound counteracts the stigma, but the stigma looms. I couldn't care less what your drive is, but I think you're drivin' into a wall. I just couldn't have Bible verse in here during the tourist season. Too risky, ya know?"

Baker remained fixed next to Bear, to look him in the eye. Bear took his foot from the stool, suddenly seeing a man void of gloom, almost glowing.

"In this bar," Baker began, arms akimbo, "we pray for a particular result. And the strength of our effort enhances such an outcome. Through the trials and the failures, we exercise our faith. It's the only way to leave as stronger men."

Baker looked to his bandmates, who had stopped what they were doing to listen to their impeccable captain. "Every gig is a chance to spread our influence. And your assumption is correct, our influence isn't far reaching, but our goals are not insurmountable. You might have to understand the process in order to perceive our quest. The effects of what we choose to do seem plain to you now, so you might see failure for us in the future. That's okay. We get that all the time." Baker returned to wrapping cords under his elbow, over his thumb. "To glorify the Lord is not an idle task. We'll move on for want of one thing, a wish to bring His word to the masses. And, Bear, one thing is clear to me—we will receive what we earn, no more, no less. And that sounds fair to me."

Moby slid out of his dilapidated, peeling snakeskin boots. Throwing his stinky footwear into a far corner, he turned up the last of his motel-spun mixer. Baker was not in the room. In the absence of their leader, Moby spoke softly, "Play as awesome as you can, but if you don't close the deal, you've just wasted your time, bruh."

Dolf cupped his hands together and rested them atop his head. The dried perspiration from his intense playing made his hair stick on end, creating the impression of a man with his finger in a live socket. "If this isn't the hardest, shallowest, most finicky business I've ever come to realize. Opportunities are nowhere."

Nat leaned on the wall, arms crossed. "We jam these uncompromising originals. That's why I'm pumped up for every show. It's that artistic arrogance, the honor of maintaining a higher calling."

But how are we supposed to bring it to the people." Moby replied. "So many are neophytes to the style, man."

Moby extinguished his smoke in the residual of an afternoon beer bottle. "We just don't have the time to do all the extras. It's all we can do to staple flyers to telephone poles." He lit another. "Hell, even Denver Christian Academy canceled our gig. Apparently, we are too loud." He let out a long exhale of smoke. "Apparently, we scare them."

Realizing that even those who share a common bond with the Holy Spirit had no use for them, no one had anything else to add.

It only took an instant of silence for Dolf to feel the gravity of peace. The still of the room soon had him shifting in his seat, reaching for his chessboard.

If memory served, it was Moby's turn to oblige Dolf a game. And in seeing the impending torture of playing chess on what was now growing into a fairly nice bourbon buzz, Moby looked for a way out of the unwanted possibility.

He could go outside, but the thought of being alone with "those wild animals" freaked him out. He could fake drowsiness, but everyone knew him not to be the first off to bed. The last resort could be a long stay in the bathroom. This would surely not be looked upon in suspicion, for Moby was the notorious king of that throne. But the door was shut. Baker had gone in fifteen minutes ago and hadn't been heard from since. No sink had run, no flush heard—Moby only stared at the door in distress.

Baker sat on the lid of the toilet, hiding his worry, the grimace that contorted his face. He leaned over his lap, doubled over, rubbing his joints, trying to settle the spasms.

His mind swam in a Demerol stupor, groping for thoughts that would take his mind away from what he had just swallowed. The voices from the other side of the door had ceased, and upon his hazy regard of the dead air, Baker knew he had been gone too long. He could feel his friends' eyes pressing on the door and sensed their apprehension, afraid to knock to see if he was all right. Baker had asked them, pleaded with them, never to acknowledge his injury, and they were complying with beautiful obedience.

They would leave their guitar player alone with his burden, the way he wanted it, and their unfailing respect made Baker smile through clenched teeth, for in his solitary distress, no one was let inside—save for one young boy, who forever remained ageless and angry, stuck in a snapshot of clear recall. He had greeted Baker, his victim, with hostility, and been called to by his kid-partner in crime, and the nickname—Zo—had rung in Baker's ears since that night. Zo . . . under a drowning veil of rain . . . Zo. Baker felt the wounds as if they were fresh, unable to stop the bleeding—f-u-c-k-i-n-g Zo.

3

ZO

As if walking through a rift in space, the picturesque conch houses with their stately gables and wide wraparound porches were suddenly supplanted by an economic polarity most locals avoided with intention. Suddenly, concrete block and mortar replaced the finest boatsman carpentry. Failing rooftops and rusty lawn furniture looked to be unorthodox amid the palm trees and vibrant hibiscus. A half-hinged door banged closed, opening once again to the beckon of the breeze.

It was an anomaly of Key West not mentioned in any travel brochures. Neighborhoods like these aren't cited on the front page of the local paper, in the *Weekender* under "Places to See, Things to Do." This was Down on Uptown, far enough sequestered from the celebrated tourist locales as the "lost borough," separated by three blocks and a barricade of like-minded opinions not to go any further, "it's just not safe." But for those who dwelled on the other side, the subjective border created the universe for those inside. It was here under a tin roof, by the hand of the midwife so busy this time of year, that Lorenzo's life began.

With four older brothers to raise, Lorenzo's mother's love was diluted. The boys were her "babies" but they were not intentional, as childbirth was often the result of careless acts between careless partners. The consequence being sons and daughters of broken homes, children running the sandy streets knowing only one side of their lineage. Most knew well of who was their father, as he likely lived around the block, across the street. But as a child developed the awareness of their own insignificance, he felt the brunt reality that their fitting love for this stranger was extinguished before an ember could ever form.

Other than redundant trips to the corner market for necessities, the village diet consisted of fish caught in the shallows or the occasional blue crab drawn to a festering chicken wing on a string. Fowl were let to roam free within the barricades of the trailer park and multiply. Hens were either preserved to lay eggs or killed by a quick hand, their necks snapped and feathers plucked in preparation to roast over open fire. Slid from the spit, the main course was often served in a festive celebration on the beach's westernmost outskirts, an area vacationers looked upon with uncertainty, a heedful trepidation before turning back to the manufactured safety of resort life and predominantly "white" numbers.

It was on the fringe, where the last steps of white sand met the wood slat barriers, where no-trespass signs marked the beginnings of the grassy pocked scrub and shrub dunes, protection for the mud turtles and marsh rabbits. Though, such a mandate meant little to the residents of Down on Uptown, as a cooked rabbit tasted so good in lemon juice and olive oil.

From here, the plinky vibe of one steel drum echoed into the endless night's black water.

The music was held in the magic hands of Lincoln, the oldest and wisest of the village. A Rasta-Christian and proud element of the Ethiopian Orthodoxy, Lincoln deftly bounced his sticks off the forged metal in a reggae anthem that was known to everyone, casting an enchanting harmony across the shore. And as the village raised their praising hands high, reciting lyrics in hypnotic reverie, Lincoln would pass the sticks to a slight boy known as Lorenzo, who kept the narcotic of impeccable sound intact through the young mind of Lincoln's oft-proclaimed prodigy.

Once Lorenzo first dropped the sticks into the well of such divine resonance, a boy at the age of eight took to the drum with such a childlike excitement that Lincoln felt compelled to teach. He saw it as nothing less than a sign from above, to take the boy under his wing, catechize him on the precepts of instrument and nature and their binding ties to one another.

Out of respect and interest for Lincoln's philosophy, Lorenzo took the place of student, absorbing an education not taught in schools, not born from another but from within, only coaxed by the master of life's great experience. But in the village, an education was a foreign concept, even considered "punk" to assimilate in such a way. It was not expected and, therefore, not important.

At twelve, Lorenzo felt the pull each time he saw his boyhood generation running off in the opposite direction, in the carefree bliss he craved. Over a few short months, hours spent with Lincoln became minutes, and minutes decomposed into precious seconds.

Ultimately, the vigor of adolescence prevailed and Lorenzo sprinted off for the last time, sand spitting from underfoot up onto Lincoln's gangly old legs. But Lincoln only smiled through his long white beard, showing yellowed teeth, knowing he couldn't and shouldn't try to hold the unbridled energy of youth any longer. He had other things to consider, and in looking out over the waters about his home, he prayed to his Lord and Savior, knowing he was only days away from transcending time and space on the journey to the everlasting, for the messenger was about to go home.

The boys of the village forever searched for a distraction from the repetition of the summer's blinding sun, the unvarying backdrop of the streets. The picture postcard of beach splendor was mundane to the children who knew of nothing else. To them, the days ran together like the tide, unvarying, monotonous, only broken by the presence of a storm cloud, bringing the episodic storms of difference, a tangent from the norm.

Down on Uptown was a hard life. The underpinnings of force to subsist, to gain leverage were pervasive. And emotions went to the edge. There were binding friendships, but with equal potency a child's mind could suffocate in anger, distrust and depression. Such a life caused a lessened state of humanity among the youth to match the four-square blocks they occupied. It was this vulnerability that caused restlessness. Perhaps this was why the basketball court was abandoned for a new sport. As bare-knuckle boxing held a promise of achievement, however temporary. Shirtless and shoe-less, the boys soon embraced the fight as daily recreation. Filling the void of brokenness by breaking another. For to win or to lose, the consequence was tangible. To the victor brought pride, to the vanquished a shame that was familiar anyway. There was simply much to gain and little to lose.

The boys old enough to take part forever wore their battle wounds: eyes swollen shut to open days later, revealing the redness of damaged blood vessels; noses broken to grow back crooked; teeth lost; ribs cracked. Though such a price was probable, most couldn't wait to prove their bravery, to get back into that circle that was freshly etched out in the sand each day by the heel of a child. Within this pint-sized ring, a rift appeared, where one passed into a certain manhood, rising up to be noticed above all else as the "baddest motha fucka" around. And upon the mastery of all who would challenge, no laurel, no medal, no first-place ribbon need be presented;

the recognition was obvious, the accomplishment considered second to none. And only one had held the title since the first ring was drawn: Malik, Lorenzo's oldest brother.

By the time Malik was thirteen, his voice had cracked its way into a low pitch, an acoustic domain of masculinity that attracted girls who were years older, and boys drawn to the dominance of his tone. At fourteen, he owned the musculature of a man; by fifteen, his rage coalesced with his superior size.

Malik chose who fought whom, and when it was his turn to battle, he pointed to older boys, those with similar physiques, for they were potential threats, and threats were to be beaten upon with the reckless fury of a young man possessed. Malik owned a bloodlust that was merciless, not stopping the fight until it was on his terms, until his opponent was damaged to the point of never entering the circle again.

The children were separated into a different division. Most were undernourished and habitually thin. But Lorenzo was also tall for his age, leaving him lanky to a greater extent. He wasn't enthused about the new hobby taken on by his peers but chose to reluctantly participate rather than live life as an outcast where there was no escape from being steadfastly reminded what you were.

His bouts usually didn't last long. Lorenzo's frame left him open for too many shots. Thinking to cover his pummeled kidneys, he would lower his defenses and get caught with a wild roundhouse that buckled his antelope legs, leaving him prostrate, coming to much later to the cool waves at high tide lapping against his aching head.

The girls watched each fray with equal anticipation. Sitting front to back with one another, they intertwined each other's long black hair into inventive chains of braids. It was an artistry taught to them by the elders, who wore twists that took hours if not days, embroidered in cowrie shells, black pearls, anything to spice up the elaborate competition among them. These women took pride in the only pastime to last through the years, passing the craft down to the children, hoping enough would embrace the tradition and keep it rooted in the ancestral sands of a proud heritage. While the skill was offered to any with an interest, the lion's share of the attention was given to one special young girl, Nina, a child who was quickly found to carry the gift in her fingertips and, more significant, an intent fascination and the patience required for such a time-consuming pleasure.

It was during one normal blistering summer afternoon, a time when Lorenzo once again found himself flat on his back with legs rolled up underneath him, when Nina, a child of his same age, approached. Breaking free from braiding up a sister with her latest conjured idea, she wanted to give a little advice to a boy she was beginning to feel so sorry for.

"Why you let'em hit'choo like that?" she asked, resting her hands on her slight hips.

The fog lifted and Nina came into view. "What'choo talkin' 'bout? Leave me alone. Don't need no girl over here tellin' me how'ta fight."

Nina pulled on the knot that tied up her soiled T-shirt, revealing her rib cage, a dark thin belly. "Somebody need to tell ya or ya ain't gonna see yo' next birt'day."

Lorenzo rose to brush himself off. Nina lent unwanted assistance by slapping the sand that he could not reach off his back.

"What'cho problem? Get away from me, girl!"

Nina backed off, putting her hands back on her hips. "You know you got somethin' those otha boys ain't."

"And what might that be, sista?"

"Them long-ass arms'a yours." Bobbing and weaving, Nina demonstrated a technique. "You should use them skinny thangs hangin' there to jab, keep 'em off ya."

"Shi, girl, that circle's too damn small. You step outta it, the otha guy get a free shot."

"So what should you do about it, Zo?"

Living on such a limited tract, everyone knew everyone's name, but Lorenzo was taken aback that she'd used his nickname, a sobriquet only adopted by his closest friends. Suddenly realizing his situation, he looked around to see if anyone had noticed this extended conversation with a "girl," well known in complex juvenile rule to be taboo if ever running over a few quick sentences. To Lorenzo's relief, the coast seemed clear. But Nina remained fixed, not budging until he asked for her offering. Trying not to relinquish his put-off demeanor, Lorenzo was forced to give in. "Well, why don't'choo tell me, o' warrior princess?"

Nina caught the nervous posture in Lorenzo growing with each word. She sensed him at an impasse, unable to get rid of such undesired attention. Confident she had won her little game, Nina began to walk away down the beach. From her silhouette, now darkened in lead of the setting sun, she tendered her advice. "Try beatin' all them otha boys down here and make yo' own circle."

As the village slept, Lorenzo went to the beach, to cut his own circles in the sand and practice his jab under the lonely glow of dawn. To avoid immediate suspicion, he composed the ring just inches bigger at first, closer inland as to avoid the breeze's ability to erase his work. In a few weeks, Lorenzo had the diameter extended by two feet.

The earlier starts to the day were difficult at first, but he kept it up, for it was pain that was at stake, enough of a reason to maintain the scrupulous regiment. And it began to pay off. The shadow boxing had increased his speed, his balance over the giving sand. Although Lorenzo was still not winning many bouts, he was able to at least step out of the ring with most of his faculties intact.

And Nina would always be there to witness the outcomes, often venturing out at first light as well, hiding in the bushes, quietly snickering while she watched Lorenzo punch at the air, at his invisible adversary.

After another midday match that lasted fifteen min-utes, for there were no rounds, no timepieces to keep track,

Lorenzo limped down to the water to rinse his mouth of the blood that trickled from his lower lip.

"You betta," said Nina, who approached him with no concern for anyone taking notice.

"I don't know what'choo been watchin', but my ass is still ova here a'bleedin.'"

Nina put a tender hand on his back, which still heaved in exhaustion. "Give it time, Zo, give it time. Then when you stawt winnin', you'll know who saved you."

With that, Nina left him to fix himself in preparation for a contest later that evening.

As time passed, Lorenzo won more and more of these beachhead donnybrooks, now becoming qualified as a reputable fighter and earning a long-overdue regard among both friend and foe. No longer were his opponents so quick to challenge, knowing full well they would get marked good by the rat-tat-tat of quick jabs, a wild scrawny elbow to the jaw. Without the constant onus of having to prove himself, of having to indulge anyone and everyone's test, Lorenzo spent more time away from that ominous circle that had stared back at him with each renewed day.

It wasn't a good idea to follow the girls around. It was regarded as being soft. In a hamlet that held no room for tender thoughts, it was risky to display such interest. But Lorenzo began to heed things about Nina, things that made him feel queasy, unnatural. And Nina, with her coquettish manner in full exploit, paid him no mind at all, for the chase was on and she had the ball. Nothing more than a few curt glares and a nose in the air kept the game interesting. Nothing more than playful flirtations continued over the next year.

The children of Down on Uptown came of age, maturing at a galloping pace, which came from having to learn to walk almost at birth. And over such a time, certain feelings between Nina and Lorenzo began to evolve.

Nina felt more the flattery of Lorenzo's attention. She let her guard down with more regularity, allowing frequent moments of her time. The childhood years had been hard but also kind to Nina, sculpting her body ever so gracefully. Through beauty and an unflinching self-confidence, Nina, at twelve, had established herself as a figurative queen among girls and could have any boy. But reverence was something she had come to realize. She knew her feelings for Lorenzo had been planted years before and were taking to a deep, strong foundation of blooming legitimacy.

Spending long afternoons under shady palms, swim-ming naked in the moonlight, they explored each other's body. Stumbling fingers learned a soothing caress. Soft kisses led to amplified emotions. But Nina would not yet allow Lorenzo to go any further. She had lived as one of eight brothers and sisters. She had seen what attending to such a rabble was like and wanted no part. Nonetheless, they were bound together in the bliss of lover's content, two soul mates amid the minus-cule environment they called home.

Lorenzo cherished this new feeling beating away in his chest, never wanting to endanger this affinity by being greedy, self-indulgent. For most of his peers, the developing female was held up as a prize, a trophy. To Lorenzo, however, Nina was so much more. She was part of him, the most important part. And he took care of her the best he could.

They spent every precious moment together within the innocence of young love. Lorenzo, forever thoughtful, heeded Nina's each and every unconscious need, to more than simply dote upon her beauty but respect her strength. And so Lorenzo listened as well as spoke, hindering none of Nina's aspirations that rose above what was understood in the village as "the woman's place." For Nina, such simple considerations were enough. But Lorenzo wished for the ability to buy her gifts, pretty things for her to adorn, lifting his love, if only psychically, above that of her beautiful but humble essence.

His mother demanded that he not mix with the whites, stay put between the streets that outlined his domain. But Lorenzo began to picture these boundaries to be like prison walls, hooded with rolling spirals of sharp barbwire. But with such a mixture of curiosity and defiance swelling by the day, he would disregard her rules, thinking, who was she to suddenly start giving a damn what he did? Lorenzo had seen Marcus leave for Sunset, to sell conch shells from a shopping cart. And Raphie was knotting shirts, dipping them in buckets of tie-dye to peddle on Duval. His twin brothers were only thirteen, a year older than Lorenzo. If they could become more naturalized to the area, making money in such conventional ways, why couldn't he?

It was the end of the month, the day Lorenzo's mother rose early to pull the welfare check from the mail. Welfare day was shop day, and Lorenzo volunteered for the task. As the screen door squeaked to a close, he received the one steadfast edict from his mother's bedroom. "Don't forget my lotto, Lorenzo! Gold Rush Double, baby, Gold Rush Double!"

It was a place he had been to many times before, but never before carrying such a desire to see more. Today he would skip the ramshackle ghetto market, the redundant aisles of Froot Loops and pork rinds, Slim Jims and Swisher Sweets, the dusty Key West souvenir shot glasses, and fried chicken gizzards aside a jar of floating pickled eggs.

The contemporary markets were eight blocks up and three blocks over. Sweat dripped from Lorenzo's chin as he finally reached the corner of Truman and Duval. Waiting for traffic, he lifted one foot and then the other, easing the inflammation caused by hot asphalt on the exposed flesh poking through the holes in his sneakers.

Crossing the street, he watched as a white woman with silvery hair exited the store that was his destination. A child pedaling his bicycle too fast down the sidewalk flew across the open market doorway. The woman showed surprising balance as she whirled out of the way, barely missing his handlebars, losing only a few of the contents that she carried. In witness to the near collision, Lorenzo approached to help gather up some oranges and limes, which had rolled off the top of her overflowing shopping bag.

She was all too grateful, charmed by this boy's courteous nature. As the last of the produce was replaced, she shook the young boy's hand. Maybe she held it a bit too long, feeling the calluses, the knuckle bones out of place. She saw a scar over his upper lip, a nose that had obviously been broken. A look of pain, then concern, crossed her face.

"What is your name, young man?"

"It's, uh, Lorenzo."

"Nice to make your acquaintance, Lorenzo. My name is Beatrice Smerconish, but most folks around here call me Aunt Bea." She took a step back, putting her finger to her lips in thought. "You know, not to be forward, dear, but I am looking for some help at my guesthouse, a little bed and breakfast a few blocks away. Some cleaning, landscaping, odd jobs. My husband and I are getting a little old, you see, to do all the tasks that keep our inn so special."

"You wanna hire . . . me?"

"Why, yes, Lorenzo. I'd like to give you the opportunity. Are you interested?"

"Well, yeah. I mean, when do I stawt?"

"How about Monday morning. But . . ." Aunt Bea moved her finger to her chin, shaking her head slightly at the sight of his draggled T-shirt, his oversized basketball shorts. "Those clothes just won't do, dear. I have some things in the attic you should fit into just fine. My grandkids grew out of them years ago, but I just couldn't part with the memories, you see."

Aunt Bea stepped toward Lorenzo, giving him a squeeze to his shoulder. "We'll get you all set up. Here's my card with the address. Seven in the morning, okay?"

Lorenzo didn't even think to ask how much he would be paid. Thinking only of money in his pocket, he accepted the offer.

Lorenzo would leave and return to the village in his old clothes. Halfway to the guesthouse, he kept a bag of three-button shirts and linen pants, white-boy outfits that would have his butt kicked into the next month if the fellas ever saw him in them. Behind a grove of cabbage palmettos, he would strip down and assume the new role, feeling a bit queer at first. But in a way, he felt a sense of purpose, and over time, the strange attire began to lose its stigma. He was clean, at least on the outside, causing a growing sense of pride, easing the ill-fitting feeling of the hidden identity, the "little white lie" he kept from everyone.

And so it went, Lorenzo pedaling off each morning on a beachcomber provided by Aunt Bea to work in a part of town Nina could only visualize in her mind. Though, no matter how colorful Lorenzo's descriptions could be, it left her overall conception blurred. She needed her own personal version of her home in total, becoming more suscep-tive toward the unrelenting itch to see more.

Her days without Lorenzo felt recklessly empty. She won-dered more and more about the short-timers who frequented her end of the world. A few extra footsteps could take her farther east down the beach, to the place where masses of people came to "get away from it all." *Away from what?* she pondered.

She rarely mingled about the tourists, only going out of her small sphere with head lowered, hunting for seashells to adorn her braids. But this time, she would turn her attention to the goings-on around her. Nina stepped off the street and hugged the coastline, walking slowly until she arrived at the most populated segment of the beach. Upon taking in the newfound interest of her surroundings, what Nina found were scores of tourists both pale and tan set up in what looked to her like miniature campsites across the vast expanse of sand. Some tested the ocean's depth to thigh level before jogging back to dry land. Others walked the waterline, fleeing from the oncoming surf as if it might bite. And there were those who never left their colorful beach towels, lying back for hours like patient wayfarers, gripping the terry-cloth edges as if it would soon take off like some kaleidoscopic flying carpet.

Outlining the beach was a broad sidewalk littered with vendors selling a variety of lunch foods. It was there, just steps from their purchase, where burgers, hot dogs, gyros, and tacos doused with saucy extras might run down the faces and chests of the children, or the more obese adults. These were the antics that went round and round in an endless cycle, all adding up to a certain ecstatic oblivion Nina couldn't quite understand. "Why all dese white people come here to do a bunch'a nothin'?"

For the next few days, Nina sat on a rock wall waiting for something to happen, but it went on and on, different people with the same idea of a jolly good time. She was ready to pursue a new direction, when Nina noticed a woman in alabaster skin spreading her towel on what certainly was her first day under the Florida sun. Much later, the sunbather awakened from a nap to find herself reddened from hours below the harsh rays of near-cloudless Southern daylight. Poking at her body in horror, she fled in haste, leaving everything behind to tend to her burns.

Nina watched as a shadow floated over the area where the woman had lain. There, a book's pages flipped in the wind beside the vacated towel, as if a midday spirit had decided to undertake an afternoon of speed-reading.

Nina gawked at the fluttering pages. She had never stolen anything in her life, but she was ashamed of her ignorance, her third-grade reading level. A rush of excitement overcame Nina, motivating her to read that abandoned book, cover to cover, no matter what it entailed. She would absolve herself of the crime, chalking the deed up to furthering her education. Nina sat perched like a tiger ready to pounce on her enticement as soon as the shadow moved on.

The pages told of a playwright who lived in a place called London. According to the introduction, this book contained a collection of his most famous work. Nina held the book close, hiding it, embarrassed to be seen with such a large composition. Each night, she would retreat to the sanctity of her hideout in the bushes, to read endlessly through the sequence of "this guy Shakespeare's" work. She read fast through the words too old to understand in an effort to get the feel of an overall sentence, drawing upon her own contrived meanings, which were always a keen hypothesis of what William truly meant. She read aloud over and over again for better recognition, enjoying the comedies, the antics of Puck or "Tri-Trin-coo-lo," but preferring tragedy, Romeo and Juliet in particular.

As Nina and Lorenzo's friends grew older, the beach became less significant. A bad impression had been drawn over the years as a stretch of time pulled memories away from Lincoln's hymnal vibe, bringing about a feeling of discomfort, making them subconsciously want to flee the only place that was natural, impeccably flawless. Those too old to aspire for anything better stopped feeling compelled to the water's edge, remaining invisibly constrained to rusty lawn chairs just a few feet from the arch of their doorways, content to bitch about lives going nowhere, blaming any and all in bitter revelry.

But Nina started to see things in a different light. She began to take extrasensory pleasure in all its offerings. The sand seemed to rise and fall like the breath of a companion, like one who had always been there, sitting quietly, listening in satisfied observation as the boys and girls became men and women, moving on to procreate a new generation, which the shore would gladly chaperone from dawn to starry night.

And Nina read on, the same fat paperback, over and over. Entire plays were committed to memory. The vast expanse of scalloped sand became her stage. And following an act where she portrayed everyone, Nina would swear to hearing the faintest applause emanating through the blowing grains, beckoning her to go on. Always with a proud bow, she continued to perform in solitary involvement. Here, alone under a curtain of twilight, a young girl with no social standing grew to love the stories of this man who, in the beginning, so long ago, had no social standing.

Nina had all but forgotten about her brother's gift, a tattered map that had been given to her before his departure, for Thomas was the only member of the family who had the mettle to leave penniless in search of something better. And for this, he was considered a traitor, a pariah, for his lack of devotion to what he was, where he was from. The village could only resolve their own complacency by judging him guilty, guilty of running away, knowing deep down his only crime was being braver than any dared.

At first, Nina never opened it, apprehensive to see what the big picture was like. That's how Thomas put it, "The Big Picture." Little did she know what that meant until her new-found interest in learning prompted her to take it out from under her bed, take it down to the beach to unfold, laying rocks on each corner for stay against the sea breeze.

This map spoke volumes to Nina. She found how little, how remote was her place, circled by Thomas, and so big was the country. She whispered, "Is that green area really that green, green and flat as far as the eye can see? Are those mountains as tall as Thomas said? How high is fo-teen thousand five hundred and twenty-two feet above sea level?" Nina looked out over the ocean. "This must be sea level." She looked to the sky. "Shoo, that's up there." It took Nina several attempts before she figured out how to refold the map. Once this obstacle had been conquered, she pulled it out regularly.

The daily routine of his job was never part of Lorenzo's repertoire as he rehashed his experiences outside the village to Nina. His employer was a sweet old lady—the "salt of the earth," as one guest described her. And she looked after Lorenzo, providing for him whenever she felt the need, and paid him right on time.

But once his occupation was uncovered, Lorenzo could not escape what his brothers had spelled out in no uncertain terms—that his position was that of a slave, an opinion that wore down every gratifying thought he had formed toward his livelihood, assurances that once gave him pride in a job well done, and it shook him where he stood.

His older siblings replaced "Zo" with "Uncle Tom," playfully mimicked by Nina's five-year-old sister, who chimed in just to be in on the tease, knowing nothing of its significance. The interpretation from those he looked up to forged a path straight to his heart, and Lorenzo began to see things in a different way. On the job, he became sensitive to every minute detail, like a pat on the head after changing soiled bedsheets or tending to clogged toilets. The flagging eye contact upon serving key lime pie to the guests became a disconsolate reminder that banged upon Lorenzo's spirit. But to see Nina's eyes light to the simplest bequests of a summer dress or abalone earrings sent any offensive thought reeling miles off to sea.

Though unbeknownst to Nina, some of what he provided was now used, owned by those same visitors who, Lorenzo perceived, looked down their noses at him, who discounted his pathetic existence—he was sure of it. Such thievery was wholly justified, treble damage in retaliation to the outright racism and disrespect he imagined each day. Suddenly, not even boxing victories made him feel so much like a man. Once proud of his solitary-if-wearisome endeavor to succeed and have money in his pocket, Lorenzo now fancied "gettin' over on the crackas." After all, his big brothers thought it was all too cool.

Another year passed and Lorenzo hadn't missed a day, huffing back to the B and B at dawn for more alleged psychic abuse answered by the retaliatory petty theft, all the while not knowing his path had already been chosen. Each of his older brothers had chosen it, as well as all but one of Nina's. Malik was again in charge, with three brothers at his side to foster the dealings that had become so amazingly profitable, drawing in every impressionable boy with dreams of having enough wealth to rise above his crummy existence.

During one weak moment, a dark figure on a pale horse had ridden into Down on Uptown, to turn a community formerly built on a coexistent pride into a void of surrendered souls, taken over by the vulnerability of the disenchanted hungry youth, spoiled by the physical and mental dishonesty cocaine and drug money had induced upon their undeveloped minds.

4

INFLUENCE

The Shade rose to prominence quickly. Under Malik's leadership, they soon spread their dealings from the local contingent of "Mary's," buskers and artisans, north to the greyhound track, hooking throngs of addicted personalities who could always use another vice. They drove up the island chain, dropping product to trusted middlemen. Dependencies were formed, and the cash flow was growing. But it was trite compared to what the young slangers of Down on Uptown would soon encounter.

A customer base came to town poised to launch the gang into unfathomed wealth. Spring break was a stretch of overindulgence, when every waking moment was spent with drugs and drinks. Undergrads poured into the island in a matter of hours, leaving an ill-equipped police force too bewildered to do anything against such a determined mob. They moved in hungry masses up and down the beach, the main drags, maintaining an unleashed passion to binge, to be as uncivilized as they wanted to be, bashing the gays, pissing in alleys, vandalizing at will.

The sudden increase in user frenzy led to a heavy recruitment within the village. The girls were frowned upon as members, thought of as little more than vehicles for sex. The young men, however, especially those with ties, were considered inherently loyal, conscripted to build on gang law, gang order.

Consequently, the first to be initiated were immediate family, and like with the detested boxing circle, Lorenzo was again faced with what rejecting such a popular proposition would bring. To be exiled from friendship was one thing, but expatriation from the family was inconceivable. He couldn't imagine the fallout of being dropped by Malik and Harold, the big brothers he held in such high esteem for being nothing more than . . . big brothers. And when all boys over the age of ten jumped at the chance to be initiated, Lorenzo, creeping up on his fourteenth year, saw himself standing alone, weighing potential outcomes that resulted in only one decision. It wouldn't take lavish enticement. The negatives of opposing the movement were too much to stomach. Lorenzo was in.

He was taken on as a "hook." Malik provided his freshest recruit with a shiny new oxblood-red beachcomber with three speeds and a hand brake, on which Lorenzo pedaled the main streets, covering as much ground as possible to connect with the public.

Malik's business was planned with caution. He kept loyal contacts on every corner, but even with such convenient accessibility, the bravest or drunkest of the collegiate crowd would drive their convertible Mercedes or their souped-up Camaros into the village with tops down, windows open, and cash in hand, searching diligently for someone who held what they needed. And there, sitting just outside the arc lamps' glow, the stoutest of the boyhood ring would wait, looking for the opportunity to lash out a wild fist that might catch the passenger on the chin, startling him enough to grab big bills from a momentarily loosened grip.

To retaliate led to a risk of grave possibilities. To chase the young thief would prove perilous, as others hid around fences and behind cars like a pack of dogs, ready to back their "brother." Days later, a young man might wash up on the shores of Marathon, flown home to a dumbstruck mother who would wonder how such a thing could happen to her "innocent" boy.

But they dared nonetheless, for they had never experienced such a superhuman feeling of self-importance, an impudent nature that shed the skin of a better angel in favor of a deviant. Students living so far from the ocean had never experienced *this* cocaine, if ever acquainted with it at all, and they watered at the mouth for more, happy to pay any amount, running off to share the secret of a drug that seduced you to love yourself more.

And like a spread of the latest campus gossip among the fraternal collective, cocaine filled the minds of the weeklong visitants with one single-minded craving.

Lorenzo's bicycle became a beacon for any who ran dry or might want to see what all the fuss was about, not wanting to be shut out of the cool thing to do. Business got to a point where he had to line the "suckas" up in wait for his return. Lorenzo was earning in fifteen minutes what he made in a week as a "slave" and at once became addicted to his welfare, devotedly working from sundown on Mallory Square to daybreak outside the fully booked hotels. It wasn't long before he was embraced by the bosses and lifted to the responsibility of overseeing the younger workforce.

To maintain such a dogged work ethic, Lorenzo needed an occasional boost. He began to dip into his delivery, coating his gums for an instant of energy. After all, it was there for the taking and Malik expected as much, for "skinchin'" on the whites was a rule found to be all too easy to follow. Most couldn't tell on sight the correct weight anyway, nor would they ever dare to question. Lorenzo was told to just pack it up if ever interrogated on quantity. Once one step went toward the door, they always backed down.

For Lorenzo, what was a sporadic remedy for fatigue grew into a fixed passion. He was now taken seriously by the same brothers who paid him no mind as a kid while making more money to buy his Nina finer things. He was on top of the world. How ironic that it was the same way the Spring Breaker felt when they indulged. But they would soon return to school, working toward some loftier goal, while Lorenzo moved from the prison of the island to the dungeon of addiction. Superiority emanated from a small young mind that was not at all at peace but bounced off walls just like that of the weakest cokeheads he dealt with night after night.

When heroin was incorporated into the product line, Lorenzo took to the new drug practice with equal intensity. The heat wave coursing through Lorenzo's body after a speedball injection contained a certain euphoric contention that quickly pushed the method of snorting lines into a pastime demotion. Never having to wait through any time lag before the drug kicked in and never waking up with a sore blood-dried nose were absolute benefits. The excitement over the fresh high flooded into every thought of the Shade. It wouldn't be long before the relief of getting a fix, just to feel normal again, shoved all other thoughts aside.

Amid the hyperactivity of drug use and capital influx, Nina had become a sideline fancy. She had avoided indulging, rather watching from afar, observing the seesaw tendencies of the addicts like a slow-motion nightmare, fully aware her lover was slipping further away into his habit. Their meetings became superficial. Nina tried bringing Lorenzo down to earth, but when grounded, the ache to fill his vein grew intolerable.

Lorenzo felt humiliated each time he fixed in front of her, each time her eyes weighed heavily upon one of his sessions as to make his skin crawl. But the guilt was now so thin it merely bugged him like a pesky gnat. To ease his disgrace, Lorenzo would offer Nina a hit, just to shoo the annoyance away. That's what Nina had become to him, an unnerving anomaly that just didn't fit into the scheme of things, a defiant who Lorenzo wished would just take his needle in her hands so he could love again.

These endless propositions pounded on her defenses. All Nina wanted was to have him back. But she was reluctantly seeing that things could never return to those days of boring simplicity, where the only agenda involved her Lorenzo and little else. With a patient and persevering outlook of happy endings growing more and more impossible to attain, depression set in, her strength diminished to a submissive state. She imagined the only way to reach him would be to share in his livelihood, in this drug that now put her a so-distant second.

Inside Down on Uptown, the addiction was a contrast to the normal junkie. They were the dealers, so life could function more coherently, knowing they controlled the arrangement of the next session. Coming off the extreme of the high was less unnerving, knowing they wouldn't need to look far for more, wouldn't need to sell their possessions, rob a store, prostitute themselves.

Lorenzo had money, and he still had the street business to run. These remained tangible connections that would become loosened with each passing day. Though a year from his sixteenth birthday, Lorenzo traded in his bike for a black Mustang with centerlines and impenetrable tinted windows, and a Beretta

9mm. Nina embraced her own delusive happiness with equal enthusiasm, buying clothes she would have never worn a few months ago, piercing her nose, belly button, and labia.

They were together again, if only meekly linked through the haze of waning mental clarity. But it felt like a bond welded solid, never to break again. At least that's how it appeared through Nina's tunnel vision, her dilated pupils, as her map lay tattered in the corner, becoming a means for the rats to line their nests.

The success of the Shade filled Malik with paranoia. Haunted by the potential for a downfall, he ordered all members to remain in the village during idle time and only flaunt their new wares in private, among one another. To do otherwise was to face an unimaginable wrath at the general's hand. But no matter what new law Malik imposed, it could not compensate for the boon that was creating new gangs, formed by those beaten down and kicked out of the Shade. What was once a solitary business was now inundated with hostile competition. Combat turned from slashed tires to fists, from knives to guns, causing fates that began making ink in the local paper. Marcus was taken by a bullet to the head. Raphie had been gutted in a crosstown alley, found so much later that his blood bore a permanent stain next to the dumpster he had been thrown into.

Down on Uptown became inundated with zombies. Members of the Shade were dropping off, losing the sense of loyalty to the gang in favor of the needle as they plunged heavier and heavier doses into the bruised crux of their elbows.

It wasn't Malik's or Harold's death that altered Nina's feelings. Nor was it the demise of almost everyone she had ever known and loved. It was the vision, a phantom she met regularly through the night as she came off the heroin. Between black flashes, far from any semblance of rest, she saw her childhood, her first intimacies with Lorenzo. She remembered hours spent with Shakespeare or the world under cornerstones as she brushed the sand away to reveal new and intriguing geography.

This time on the edge of sleep was the longest period between fixes, causing a burning withdrawal on a nightly basis. Just before daybreak, Nina's gut wrenched as sweat beaded and ran down her temples. It was at this time that the future came into light.

The trepidation brought on by the sight of Lorenzo's lifeless head bobbing in the ebbing tide was originally discounted as a terrible dream. But each night, the darkness behind Nina's eyelids framed a picture of equal horror as the finale ended the same way, different only in the manner Lorenzo's demise was portrayed.

As the survivor, she felt the nightmare becoming much more distressing, for how could she go on as half the person she was, which was now only a small fraction of a person in the first place? She'd left her best attributes behind when she tied off her arm for the first time.

With the loss of Malik and Harold, Lorenzo moved up the chain of command. Anytime Cyrus, the new general, went up the coast on business, he was in charge. And under Nina's waning clarity, she was dismayed to find he embraced his role, excelling in his new capacity to rule.

Lorenzo's job began in the field, and that's where he chose to remain, not sending out messengers but dealing boldly face-to-face. Nina shivered at the thought that by teaching him how to fight in order to win respect, she may have melded her Zo into what he now was. The passive, slight boy she first knew had taken the form of a confident but tragically reckless leader, careless to consequence, and always returning to headquarters with the tunnel vision to press another dose before the "flu on steroids" got any stronger.

And as Lorenzo became busier, Nina was alone again, left with one momentous task, to fight her own withdrawal with all she had and win back her life. So Nina would walk away, to find solitary confinement, without authority over what controlled her life, without a kind hand from a sober companion, and without knowledge of the depths from which she needed to crawl. Though, Nina—the "warrior princess," as Lorenzo had imparted on her—had one touchstone against all that would bang on her innermost core: love. Love gave her the most profound purpose, an aspiration for marriage, to bear children with the one and only man she was destined to spend the rest of her life—a long life, she hoped. *Yes, a long life*, she thought as she gritted her teeth, rocking away in the dark corner of her bedroom, sweating and freezing for the two longest days of her life.

Nina felt her mind collapsing in on itself. Her thoughts bounced back and forth like a pinball between mushroom bumpers. Blinded by hot trans-lite flashes, she leaned over to vomit nothing but the smallest spit of yellow bile.

I gotta get up. Her survival instincts kicking in, she rubbed some life into her aching arms, back and forth over what had become gooseflesh. By the crutch of the bedside, Nina got to her feet, wobbling and shaking. On impulse, one foot went in front of the other, away from the village, the place where it all began, and all ended. With nothing more than a beach towel and a small satchel of untouched fruit, she took to the beach, along sand she once adored, hoping to find the solution, to manifest again her destiny, which not so long ago seemed so certain.

She recalled the small white structures on the beach, from where lounge chairs were rented. *They will be closed this time of year. It's not far,* Nina gathered, as she had been there many times before, when she was well, a fit young girl driven by curiosity. *I will break in, crawl inside, rest . . . and get back down to business.* This was no plan, just a goal, to get from point A to point B, going nowhere by going somewhere.

Nina's mind waned, propelled by thoughts already corrupted by full body pain as it collided against what hope was left. The walk on the soft sand was torture as it gave way under her feet, pushing her left, right. The wind gusted off the ocean, sand pelting her face, feeling nothing like a nuisance but like pinpricks as she wiped her face, each time looking for blood that wasn't there. Under the weight of her sack, Nina fell. She turned to look back home, discouraged at the short distance she had traveled. *I can't breathe. I can make it back. One more hit and I can try again . . . tomorrah.*

Inhaling deeply, Nina turned away, eyes forward. *No, dammit!* She shivered relentlessly as she dug one foot back into the sand and then the other. She slung the satchel again over her shoulder, feeling the canvas scrape her hypersensitive skin, back and forth, as if a dull saw blade would soon remove her limb.

Through her watery eyes, Nina looked to the full moon, trying to fixate on its glow, fool her mind, if only to have a few seconds of grace from the terror. But through her dilated pupils, the moon was too bright and seemed to singe her vision. Her nose ran without end, dripping in tandem with the sweat from her aching head. And she fell again.

To the water, easier to walk. But the water was a frightening temptation. It was an out. Too close and she may keep going, satisfy her mounting desire to die.

No longer strong enough to carry her sack, Nina let it fall to the ground. *Why am I carryin' this?* she asked herself, as any appetite seemed like such a joke. Leaving what few belongings she had, Nina rose again, stumbling toward the water.

Almost there. But what was the purpose of her direction? It was manageable, downhill. *These bugs won't bite me down there.* Closer to the water, she felt the wet sand, freezing cold.

Exhausted, she dropped a third time. Nina's head fell into her chest. *Lincoln . . . God . . . take me from this.* No longer could she hear the roar and crash of the waves. Raising her head, looking out over the surf, she saw only the beckoning of each approach, white froth reaching up to lick her fingers, beckoning her to move closer. Nina crawled out farther, and the ocean took her by the wrists, the elbows. *Soon it will be over. I'm so tired . . . so . . . so . . . tired.*

Nina was underwater, or that was the impression. After all, she couldn't breathe. But she was now floating, yet within her madness, with hypersensations bouncing from fire to ice, she felt the air on her face, the salt on her upper lip. *Am I dead?* Nina thought. She felt as if she were bound tightly, clasped around each arm, each leg, and the pain was unbearable. *This can't be what heaven feels like. This . . . this is hell.*

Looking through crazed and blurred vision, Nina saw several dark silhouettes leaning over her, faceless in the night. *Grim reapers*, she thought.

The need sent demons that tried to fool Nina into feeling she was within an inch of her life and, without another hit, it would soon be over. These demons arrived in the form of Jesty, her best friend who overdosed, seized, and died; of her mother, rocking away in perpetuated premature old age, ragging on how miserable her existence was and how Nina wouldn't amount to a damn thing; and of Malik, whose blows felt so real as they came down on Nina's face, causing her to leap off her pillow, awakening to wipe away the blood only to realize it was merely the remnants of sweltering duress.

But the elders would always be there, not the orthodox inhabitants of the village but the Rastafarians who had known Lincoln best. From afar, they had watched their community burn. They had quickly identified the enemy that took residence in their community after Lincoln's passing, electing to live as separatists until the shadow of the menace lifted from their beach. It was this party that had picked Nina up from the surf, stripping her of her clothing, layering her body in soft, loose linens.

Nina was given melatonin produced from algae to control some semblance of a sleep cycle. She was given a pumice of valerian root and calcium to control her tremors, cramps, and joint pains. Vitamin C was administered carefully down her throat through an eye dropper.

Nina had not fixed in six days, and she felt her body in recovery. She looked to her caretakers, who never seemed to stop talking, to themselves and to her. Still others appeared to be meditating, smoking marijuana and praying around her. They had been covered from head to toe in colorful garments, reds, golds, greens, and blacks. But today, the men and women adorned in white, and the one leaning over her, noticed her contemplating the change of attire.

His voice was quiet and kind, but stern. His face was passive but not dismissive. "God has endowed yuh wid an unsuspected powa of endurance, young one." With arms outstretched, he looked to the sky. "Zara, remove har bonds."

Under her wraps, Nina was naked. The men had departed, leaving women to rub lavender oil on her body, diminishing the smell created from excreting the toxins. She was helped to her feet and presented a wineskin of lemon water. Nina took the skin and began to drink.

"Careful now," chastened Zara. "Yuh bady reborn . . . likkle sips . . . only likkle sips."

The man, who Nina assumed to be her main caretaker, returned. He sat down next to her and crossed his legs. His elbows went to his knees, and his long fingers came together, steepling just under his nose. His dreadlocks were mature and long, with the front-most strands tied up behind his head. His beard had white streaks dripping down from the moustache. Despite what Nina perceived to be a man of middle age, his skin was clear, surprisingly youthful for someone living under such extreme elements.

They sat together for a moment in silence as his deep, dark eyes gazed impassively over her. And as he saw the spirit he hoped he would, his hands lowered and turned, pointing his pressed fingertips toward Nina.

"Soon di events of di imperfect world will again be force 'pan yuh. We muss learn 'ow to navigate di axis between gud and evil. Todeh wi' tek firs' steps, mi pickney, mi child."

Nina felt exhausted. But she bowed her back against the sentiment, keeping her desire to rest hidden in her upright posture. But he could read her body language, the way her fists balled up when she put her shoulders back, how the corners of her mouth drew back with every subtle move. He smiled ever so slightly. "Yuh read of a Shakespeare, dis mi know."

Nina's eyes narrowed. *How could he . . . ?*

The man put his hand on her shoulder and leaned in close. "But him simply a poet. A playwright of fantasy. But yuh, Nina, yuh are di bard of yuh own existence. Yuh wil' construct yuh future . . . an' di future begins t'dey."

He took Nina by both hands, helping her to her feet. Nina stepped forward, her legs wobbly like a newborn deer. The man kept his hand protectively on her arm. Nina paused, lowering her head and closing her eyes, clearing her mind before looking up in concentration at the sand ahead. "What is your name?" she asked.

"Mi Aaron," the man replied. "Mi did call to act 'pan yuh struggle. Dis a' all yuh need know of mi."

And it was at this point Nina realized Aaron was sent by God, through Lincoln, she surely felt. She looked out to the sand, and a small smile crossed her face. "Yeah, child," answered Aaron. "It did he."

For the next several days, Aaron helped Nina, first by being a crutch and then as a companion. He taught her thoughts to meld with the cadence of her steps, which ultimately became strides.

"Act 'pan whah 'ave been given."

"Hunga fi greata meaning."

"Tu'n tuh di things yuh luv."

Aaron met Nina each morning at daybreak. He extended their walks together each day as he brought the Lord into every intention he had for Nina's recovery. As they meditated together and practiced yoga, Aaron planted a spiritual seed in Nina, tending to his design until the framework affixed itself to her thoughts. At dusk, Nina sat with Aaron and the Bible as he described the story in conceivable terms, in a cathedral of lessons that grew into legitimate truth.

Nina was struck by Aaron's devotion and came to find his reasoning to be the foundation of what would save her. Her physical strength was necessary. To practice in the honing of her body was the steel that held her up. But at the apex of the steeple, her understanding of who she grew to know so personally was the key that unlocked the cell of her psychic disgrace.

Her small victories over what seemed an endless fight under moon and sun eventually cracked the spell of compulsive want. Her brain no longer sent false messages of a physiological obligation for heroin. Her body stopped aching; her legs stopped quaking. The bridge from her pain to hope handed Nina back her sanity, propelling her, once again, to the other side. There, she found herself on a remote island, knowing no one would be waiting to welcome her back, no one left to relate to anymore, to hang with. Though this no longer mattered, it was time to make every effort to bring the one hostage she cared for back from the abyss.

Nina's final day was a celebration. The elders again wore white in honor of the King of Kings. She filled her belly with the finest ital meal of vegan porridge and rice, a papaya-and-melon smoothie.

Then she danced, no longer under the malaise of recovery, as she smiled till it hurt, not having broken into such an expression in what seemed years. As the sun kissed the ocean, Nina embraced each and every elder who had saved her, which, in shifts, was everyone.

Aaron was the last to take her in his arms, placing his bony fingers on the back of her head, on hair that had been unbraided, unbound, as soon as she was brought in. Nina remained in his embrace, and Aaron felt her mind flexing, ruminating.

"Wah' is it dat yuh desire, mi child?"

Nina stepped back, a look of conviction crossing her face. "You know me now, Aaron. In this short time, you've come to know everything about me." She paused to swallow the lump in her throat. "So you know I need to come back."

Aaron opened his arms, palms turned up. "It wi' be yuh fos' test, mi child. Him will not come suh easily. Luk to di heavens. Seek guidance in Him." He took one step forward. "But yes, Nina. Yuh bring yuh man Lorenzo. Mi wi' bi waitin'."

Nina no longer wondered how Aaron knew, for she now knew she had angels looking over her. And her face became as bright and beautiful as ever. From over her shoulder, she blew Aaron a kiss as she ran back to the imperfect world.

Days had passed. Nina stayed in hiding from the village, looking for a sign, a lit doorway to walk through and reenter the corrosive environment of Down on Uptown. Her mind grew dark as the best-laid plan stayed hidden from her. All that she loved, she loved even more, but he was deep inside the beast. Nina sat in dread, knowing there would be no sorrow, no pity, and no shame left in her Lorenzo. And the thought that all his sweetness had been squeezed from him left Nina in a trembling state of melancholy as thoughts of a damnable verdict would be his ultimate consequence.

These feelings ate at her heart, and tears glistened down her face as the first shadows of night crossed over her body. It was at this bleak moment she thought of all those who had suffered and died in the village, from the best to the worst of them. Nina realized she had pleaded to God solely to save Lorenzo, but Aaron's words suddenly came to memory: *Confess, resist, and restore, young one.*

Nina confided in God, disclosing every sin that came to mind. She had thwarted what once owned her. "What have I restored other than my own purpose?" she whispered. It was at that moment Nina felt a warm glow in her bosom, which tracked to her temples. *Under the influence, they were unable to cry out to the Lord,* she realized. And this understanding pulled Nina up onto her knees. Squeezing her hands together, she began to pray not only for herself and her love but also for the deliverance of both friends and enemies, one and all.

What was an hour seemed like minutes within her passionate appeal. When she was finished, Nina looked forward, and her eyes turned sharp, animated. The muscles in her jaw flexed. The cold sensation of doubt was gone, and her implacable purpose had returned, invigorated behind what she knew to be the shield of God. Anger and sadness became happiness, empathy. And Nina rose to her feet, not hoping to find the way but expecting it. *The Lord wills my success.*

She walked down the sands once more, looking to the sea that had taken on the appearance of liquid metal under the moonbeams. Nina hugged herself, thinking long and hard about what had intrigued Lorenzo during his innocent years. She reminisced about the days when the distance had closed between her and Lorenzo. She'd felt his eyes upon her from across the street, as if he was thinking of a safe way to approach. She recalled upon the first gift he purchased for her with his first week's pay, legitimate earnings that gave him a newfound sense of pride. It was a necklace, and hanging from the chain was a gold compass, for he understood so completely of Nina's desire to know the world around her. Before presenting it to her, he made sure to learn what lay in each direction, pointing each way toward the unknown parts of Florida, Cuba, the Bahamas, Mexico. Nina pulled her braids up and out of the way, and Lorenzo fumbled mightily with the clasp, to the point Nina felt her arm getting tired. But she could only smile in delight as he apologized over and over. Finally connecting the necklace, he'd taken Nina by the shoulders, turned her, and kissed her gently.

Nina took the compass in her hand, squeezing it as her steps continued, ruminating upon the day she first spoke to him. She seemed to feel the pain with each blow that landed on Lorenzo's face and frame. Such a sensation did not occur with the other beaten boys, only Lorenzo, for a reason she could only now comprehend as the hand of God.

Before that day, her mind was fixed on her inherited hobby, but more so hunger. This was why the best of times occurred on Saturday, when the village gathered for the weekly feast. It might be chicken, crab, rabbit, or all of it together, served with greens grown within the trailer park when the village gardened, a toil that was once a gratifying experience, before the planters were abandoned to only blossom in thistle, dandelions.

Nina could almost taste the Saturday meal. For one day a week, her appetite was satiated. It was then that she would lean back, planting her elbows in the sand, resting her full belly to the beat of the steel drum.

Yes! she thought. *The drum*! The drum always brought him into such focus. It was the look in Lorenzo's eyes when Lincoln, under his wintry dreadlocks, pointed his way for a time on the kettle. It was the private lessons, when technique was learned during a certain sermon, where Jah Rastafari was embraced amid the burdened minds of Down on Uptown.

Lorenzo was so happy to find his own inner peace through the wisdom key only Lincoln seemed to hold. For Lorenzo, the old man was as close to a father as he would know. The babbling insights given so often went well over his young mind, but when the sticks met the steel formed so carefully by Lincoln's hand, everything seemed to come together under the sun-splashed sky.

But Lincoln is dead, thought Nina. *He can be of no use to me now.*

Almost three years ago to the day, on the finest of mornings, God took Lincoln away from the physical world. Lincoln's body was buried with little ceremony, as he had requested. No other final wishes were left by word or writing. Nor was it necessary, as Lincoln owned no items of value, except one. And it was well known among the village that the bestowal of the drum would go to Lorenzo. For the boy, it would be his proudest day.

To the village's delight, he was a natural. For weeks, the Saturday feasts went on without a hitch as Lorenzo took the pain of Lincoln's departure and bottled it. As long as the sweet sounds of joviality filled the misty air, Down on Uptown was at peace. The beautiful odes to pacification gave everyone something to retain in his passing. Under a tidal wave of splendor, they gained the ability to vanquish their troubles and tear down the walls of strife, if only for a moment. To be missed and not mourned was how Lincoln wanted it, and Lorenzo fulfilled his dying wish utterly.

Maybe it was the wind, or maybe just some words formed inside Nina from what she was thinking at the time, as she became lost in the horizon, where the dark-blue waters met the light-blue heavens.

Circumstance 'ave been beatin' u'pan young Zo. One muss find di vehicle fi truth, escape dat which indentures imself tuh di beast.

Whatever may have been the case on that particular night, it was an absolute revelation, and a backing to what Nina felt she should do. Realizing she could never talk—or, for that matter, think—in Rasta, she put both hands to her lips, blew Lincoln a kiss, and ran off to find the drum.

"Baby, wake up. Wake up. I gotta show you somethin'."

Lorenzo rubbed at his bloodshot eyes, flexing his throbbing right arm in habit. "Damn, Nina, what da hell is goin' on? Are we gettin' raided or what?"

There was no sense that Lorenzo even knew Nina had been gone for what was now three weeks. Nina, in her wild desire to see Lorenzo again, was not prepared for such a cold response. She paused. A tear welled in her eye. But Nina quickly shook herself, getting back to the task at hand.

"You have to come down to the beach. There is somethin' you need to see."

"Aw, baby, can't it wait? I gotta get some z's."

Nina reached back for some forceful incentive, realizing now it would hassle Lorenzo this much to get out of bed before late afternoon. "Well here it is, Zo. Either you awaken to this beautiful new day on your own or mi a guh—I mean, I'm going to go and get some cold water to throw on your ass."

"What'd you just say?"

"Just come on."

"Shi. Where are my drawers? And my shades, definitely, where are my shades?"

Lorenzo stumbled around, tripping over a Taylor guitar case that lay hidden under a pile of clothes. He grimaced back at the black neck of the case he had kicked free. Exposed from under its hiding place, it stuck out as if to say, "Got you again, fool." Lorenzo just shook his head. Stepping into his pants, he pondered where the nearest dumpster may be.

Nina could hardly keep to a walking pace as she escorted Lorenzo off the street, toward the water.

"You gonna pull my damn arm outta its socket if you don't slow down."

"Almost there, baby."

As they broke through the foliage, the path opened to reveal what waited. Lorenzo paused, looking to the sky, visibly pissed off. "Nina, tell me you didn't jus' get my ass up at whatever time it is to play you some Jamaican groove befo' breakfast."

Nina took Lorenzo's hands in hers. "Don't you remember, Lorenzo? Don't you remember the joy it gave you to play on Lincoln's drum?"

"Sho I do, Nina, but things have changed. I ain't got no time to play that. I'm practically runnin' things around here. Watchin' everybody's ass is takin' up all my time."

Nina's posture remained rigid despite the warm tears rolling slowly down her cheeks. "Don't you think I know that? Baby, we haven't even talked to one another in more than a year. You probably don't even know I kicked that shit, do you?"

In no mood for a confrontation, Lorenzo shoved his hands into his Dickies and started back to the village. With each step, Nina's words rang out, becoming louder the farther away he became. "Lincoln bestowed upon you his most prized possession. How can you desecrate his name like this? You've lost it, Zo. The drug has given you the feeling of control, but it's weakened your mind. You've got NOTHING! That shit is gonna KILL you! IT'S KILLING ME TO SEE IT! DON'T YOU REMEMBER HOW IT USED TO BE! I LOVE YOU! I'M TRYING TO HELP YOU!"

5

SMALL MIRACLES

Nina left the drum out on the beach, covering it with care each night before bedding down. She had no worry of anyone taking liberties with it. It had been Lincoln's, and the village, knowing full well what spirits dwelled within the steel, steered well clear of its power. But the children, those who were too young to grieve Lincoln's death, had no such concern. And curiosity soon overcame a boy named Jamal, who waited until midnight before venturing down to unveil the ultimate toy.

He dragged over a large stone to stand upon. Pulling the tarp to the sand, Jamal gazed in wonder down into the concave realm of a thousand songs. The moonlight danced off the steel with an alluring glitter, enticing the boy to pick up the sticks that lay inside. Taking one in each hand, he began tapping on the forged edges, quietly at first, then harder, and harder still, unaware of the resounding tone that emanated from within.

Peering through open windows, those who heard the sound became frightened, as if Lincoln had dropped by unannounced to wreak vengeance, playing horrifically, concocting a curse on the land for leaving his beloved instrument to waste away. With such a heavy burden of guilt in their hearts, no one dared leave the safety of their doorsteps and bear witness to the reprisal of the Holy Ghost.

Lorenzo returned from a typical deal to heed the tone as well, though he was not so fearful but enraged that anyone would have the nerve to perform on his drum. He sprinted down to the beach to find Jamal swaying to and fro with eyes shut ever so tightly. "Boy, wha'choo think you doin' down here!"

The startled boy's eyes opened in terror to see the dark silhouette speeding after him. Upon reaching the rock on which Jamal stood, Lorenzo raised his hand to knock the boy as far from his roost as his swat would allow. But Jamal instinctively fell backward to the ground, sobbing for forgiveness. "I sorry, mista. I didn't mean nothin.'"

In seeing the expression of fright on the boy's soft, tender face, Lorenzo got hold of his rage but remained determined to school the boy. "Who told you you could come down here and play with dis!"

Jamal stayed rolled up in a ball. In anticipation of a backhand, he kept one arm in front of his face. "I'm sorry, mista. It was just here. It didn't look like it was anybody's! I waited to see if it was anybody's! It didn't look like it was anybody's!"

Lorenzo breathed in deeply the salty night air, slowly beginning to feel at fault, at fault for the silence, for the spider web that drew from one end of the rim, broken by the play of a little boy, to float with prophetic gesture in the wind. He rubbed his brow, trying to calm his anger further before moving over to the boy. Sitting down on the sand beside him, he turned to look upon Jamal, and it was as if he were peering into a mirror. He saw his reflection at eight years old stuck like a snapshot, and it made him crack the smallest grin. "Do you like what you hear?" he asked, now calm, under control.

Jamal perked to the question, rising to his bony, chafed knees. "Oh yes, mista, it's a fine sound."

Feeling the slightest nudge from behind, Lorenzo looked around, down the expanse of the beach. But no one was there. He paused, allowing his mind to surround the possibility that he had been touched by an old friend. Through the murk of ebbing drug effects, he nodded to the darkness. He turned back to Jamal. "Would you like to learn how to play it?"

"Oh yes, mista," spouted Jamal, fear subsiding. "Is it yours?"

"You could say dat." Lorenzo returned to stare deep into the boy's eyes as if looking for someone else in them. "I can teach you, but you gonna have to quit callin' me mista. Shoo, I'm only fifteen years old. You gonna have to call me Zo."

Jamal jumped up with the sticks still gripped tightly in his little hands. Prying them free, he offered them to Lorenzo. "Could you teach me, Zo, teach me right now?"

The music altered dramatically. Suddenly, a vibe filled the air and pounded at the heart, long missed deep in the subconscious of all who remembered. Those older, and not numbed from narcotics, began making their way down to the water, to the rim of the sea that now took on such an unearthly light.

> *And wond'ring, on their faces fell*
> *To worship that celestial sound:*
> *Less than a god they thought there could not dwell*
> *Within the hollow of that shell*
> *That spoke so sweetly and so well.*
> *What passion cannot music raise and quell!*[1]

And the village congregated once again, swaying at first and then grabbing one another to rediscover their reggae prance. No one spoke but shut their eyes in satisfaction of how things used to be, forgetting, if only in one poached moment, how drastically their lives had turned.

Nina sat on the outskirts of the bushes, watching, pulling her knees tight as if hugging her Zo for the first time in years. All her life, she had never missed the chance to move to the gesture of such a sound. But on this night, Nina chose to remain on the edge of the impromptu gathering, realizing she had a long way to go.

Members of the Shade, having lived most of their lives fatherless and in poverty, spent their windfall of drug profit

---

[1] "A Song for St. Cecilia's Day" by John Dryden, 1687.

as if it were the tireless allowance of a spoiled childhood. And Lorenzo's newfound interest in music spurred others in the gang to try their hand. But the village offered only Lorenzo's steel drum and one Taylor acoustic guitar. For reasons unknown, Lorenzo warned everyone not to touch it. So three carloads of inspired boys hit every music store and pawn shop in Key West in search of an instrument to suit. Before nightfall, their trunks were stuffed full, to hang open and flap to every bump back to the village.

They evicted several bingers from their regular tables, dragging them around like stunt dummies until half the crack bar was converted into a rehearsal space. With Lorenzo's abilities on the steel drum, the choice had been easily made to build a reggae band around him. But the process was slow. Cocaine catered to inflated confidence, keeping many clinging to the practices despite no improvement. And "horse" was an impossible handicap, as aspirations for music fell away to the compulsion for the needle.

Lorenzo, although not the general of the gang, became the leader of the band. He was the one with the special talent, the one that propelled runaway delusions of fame and fortune in the others. Though in no time, as the drug addiction trumped more passion, the fifteen who started the clamorous group soon fell off to ten, then six. Lorenzo thought five was plenty, but there was one member imposing himself on rank alone.

Cyrus had purchased a Tama kit complete with all the extras, including twenty-four-karat gold, chrome, and nickel plating. He had all the options at his beckon, a variance of sounds for his hands and feet, if only they were in synch with one another. But it was just this assortment that intimidated him, keeping Cyrus true to only the snare and bass with an occasional wild jab at the high-hat. When he was asked to incorporate another means to the beat, his cadence bounced all over the room, causing even the remaining crackheads to lift their foreheads off the table and find another place to carry on their habit. It was obvious to all that Cyrus was musically inept with little hope of improving, but no one dared lead him toward the knowledge that his play bordered on repulsive. He was the leader of the Shade and had learned all methods of retribution from Malik. A derogatory comment would prove painful if not fatal.

Trying to shut out each annoying measure, Lorenzo's eyes were fixed in admiration toward the potential of the polished equipment, the harmonious possibilities of size and sound, which he could hear despite Cyrus's inability to set up correctly, creating such a lopsided configuration as to make the true musician cringe.

The craving to try his hand behind the set thrived in his mind until he could not sit for want any longer. Lorenzo and his four other bandmates scheduled their fixes to fade at the time their general would work. Nights when Cyrus was sure to be on a deal far up the coast, Lorenzo would hold Sketchy, Flu, and the others of the group back for private sessions. He felt like a traitor the first time he took the seat Cyrus normally filled, and legitimate fear rocked his will when he first held the sticks in his hands. Lorenzo thought of Jamal sitting in the sand, shaking in preparedness for mighty blows of vengeance at his hand. But as Lorenzo had refrained from violent retribution, Cyrus would not be so sympathetic. The gang had become a business, and friendships had been wasted along with the never-ending wasted nights. But the band with no name had been bound by a fresh intrigue, a newfound excitement, which controlled their heroin craving just enough, at least until they were finished with what was now becoming more important. And like the spirit dancing steel to an innocent boy, Cyrus's drums became Lorenzo's draw. With the loyal backing he received from the others, he would risk everything.

Lorenzo picked up the contemporary percussion like a fish to water, soon forming musically astute sentences with thoughtful punctuation. He challenged the others to keep up with quick riffs and definitive stops, motivating them to pay close attention, to get inside the groove, but also making sure to play down as often—after all, it was reggae. The Rasta covers were simple beats that the five could grasp, patterning every song to Marley, Tosh, and Toots until they were driven home to be as familiar as mother's milk, played over and over until they could, in time, acknowledge their own creative flows.

The band eventually reached an impasse. Little improvement had been made. And Lorenzo realized they're hedonistic lifestyles were no longer conducive to the desire to become real musicians. "Our minds are racin' in time far too quick for a form of music in slow motion, a pace used to bring all the truth to the lyrics."

And this became the first time Lorenzo truly thought of Nina, not as a lover but as the only one who had fought off her addiction. He found her where he knew he would, sitting seaside on the dunes. She was praying softly, and Lorenzo paused. For the first time in a span Lorenzo could barely recollect, he was struck by her beauty. And his heart became heavy as the years in love washed over him. The radiance of the moon glanced across the shells that knocked like wind chimes in the braided strands that draped her shoulders, as she rocked ever so slightly, moving to the measured thoughts within her quiet solicitation to the Lord.

She had felt him there, as she would feel a part of her own body. Nina turned to look at her young man, who on this night took on a countenance of his actual age, looking almost innocent as he stood with his hands ever so deep in his pockets, at a loss for words. "Would you come sit with me?" she asked.

They spoke for hours. Even though Lorenzo's skin began to crawl with the craving, he continued, feeling an uncertain power that emanated from his long-lost love. And when the sun began to breach the horizon, he spoke the words Nina had beckoned God to bring forth. "Nina, I, uh, yeah, I'd like to try."

6

EVERY THIRD
WEDNESDAY

Denver, Late August

He put his safety goggles back into an old cotton sock and tossed them into his toolbox. Wiping sweat from his brow, Baker panned the sanctuary.

He had removed the old chancel latticework, which to Baker acted as a barrier between the priest, the deacons, and the congregation. He had extended the stage out into the nave, to enable everyone to be worshippers rather than spectators. He walked the expanse of the chancel, stepping behind the altar. Baker kept the pulpit low, for there would be little distinction between keepers and hearers of the Word, just how Father Lloyd wanted it.

Murphy had created the rails in an S curve around the altar. At Baker's request, they were made to be removable to accommodate the creative whims of Father. The rails were bronze, the balusters iron, illustrating beauty and brawn, light and heat.

The room was restored from top to bottom. The dentil work around the cornice was carefully stripped and painted, exposing once again the original architectural detail. Vandalized stained glass was removed and soldered with exact replicas, leaving no anomaly to the biblical story told on the north and south walls. Wood floors were replaced to invigorate acoustics. Eight shades of white paint, grays, and neutrals were used to give an appearance of warmth and depth, leading to the penitent purple that washed over the high expanse of the east wall.

Admiring the complete comfort of the room, Baker turned to the restored cross. He had used no electricity in framing what would be the visual genesis for all who attend. The beveled olive wood molding was not made by machine but from hours of careful taps with hammer and chisel. Once this painstaking process was complete, the cross was placed inside the sculpted wood frame and covered in gold leaf, returning from history a gilded representation of the ultimate sacrifice.

Murphy stood aside Baker as they surveyed a project almost complete.

"Usually, the craft just assumes the role of a pleasurable pastime," Baker started, slowly walking the center aisle, allowing his hand to brush over each pew in passing. "But this job, this brought out my best, our best."

Murphy followed down the aisle. "No doubt about it. It distinguished my purpose for being here."

"Here in the chapel?"

"Here on earth."

"Yeah . . . exactly."

Baker pointed through the vestibule to the double doors. "I just worked in a cadence in here . . . nothing mismeasured . . . no wrong cuts. The bubble on the level hit dead center every time. Never a doubt."

Murphy blew some debris from his glasses. "You had a definite motive, Bake. You just can't wait to bring your six-string in here."

Baker looked back over his shoulder at the guy he spent so much time with, who couldn't help but know him best. Grinning, he flexed his fingers with Pavlovian intent at the thought.

Baker sauntered down the chapel steps and into the smoggy haze of a hot Denver afternoon. He was to meet Cecil on the corner of Fifteenth and Market, at Sleeve and Jacket record store, the ultimate destination for any music lover in pursuit of a bygone era.

To Baker, LPs represented a form of purity. To a throwback like Faraday, records were symbolic of a time when it was a privilege just to edge one out of its liner.

For the last two years, Baker and Cecil had taken half of the third Wednesday of every month off. It was the day when B.A., the shop proprietor, received his largest delivery from "over the pond." The symbiotic relationship B.A. maintained with his London friends was a key element to keeping a firm ear to the ground. And those who ran indie stores long enough began to learn of "the fat man's collection" and were more than willing to trade limited-edition British Invasion for Grunge from a time before it was known to be such.

Under the looming shadow of a Virgin Records megastore, Cecil and Baker found a place so authentic. It was peaceful, far from commonplace. And B.A. always spun good tunes, so when Baker got to within view of Sleeve and Jacket, he wasn't surprised to notice Cecil ducking inside, on time as always.

The door was open, allowing the music to spill out into the street. The heat of the day may have prompted a surfer's mentality, as an energetic advertisement of Dick Dale washed over the passersby. Baker allowed his eyes to adjust to the dim inside and found B.A. where he always was, squat on a stool like Jabba the Hut behind the register. He raised one flaccid arm, pointing to his watch. "Like clockwork. G'day, my friend."

A product of the late sixties and San Francisco's Haight District heyday, he had changed his name to "Brand A" to show hostility toward big industry, oppression, the pejorative "establishment" in general. Those who knew him best called him "B.A." for short, which also had a hip meaning back in those days. To be "B.A." was alphabetically backward, "nonconformist, man," pure genius amid the loitering sloth of Golden Gate Park. Today, however, a transformed man stood before Baker and Cecil, now choosing to use the acronym for his contemporary life, for "B.A." now proudly stood for "Born Again."

He was in his midfifties, but B.A. would always be going on twenty, eating ramen and surviving on margin. His store exhibited the characteristics of the guy who had walked these floors the last twenty years. Most of the same throwback posters hung as before, blanketing nearly every bit of wall and ceiling space. The storefront windows were thick with flyers of upcoming shows. B.A.'s stable of seventies babes hung in a procession as if in a pageant, often giving rise to conversation from those old enough to remember. Farrah Fawcett's teeth looked bright as ever, but the coral red of her swimsuit and her Coppertone tan, the part of the poster exposed to years of window sunlight, had faded in stride with the memory. Loni Anderson posed in a white bikini, pushing out the attributes that made her famous. A partially torn Cheryl Tiegs was next to Suzanne Somers in a blue one-piece. She peeked from behind a corner that drooped for lack of a fourth tack.

Throughout the store, an autobiography of B.A.'s life hung in haphazard love. There were black-light posters of cobras and panthers, eighties Eschers, and nineties Magic Eyes. Lava lamps were bookends for a lightning-storm globe. Famous concert playbills were framed behind the counter, and oversized posters of Ziggy Stardust, Frank Zappa, the Clash, Iggy Pop, and the Sex Pistols intermingled within this collage spanning forty years.

To Baker's amusement, and Moby's vast appreciation, B.A. posted want ads for *Bass Guitarists Only!*, giving them a rare forum amid the dime-a-dozen drummers and guitar players, whose positions were not as difficult to fill and refill. Near these postings was a chalkboard filled with specials of the day, authoritative selections B.A. drew up new on every third Wednesday. Next to the ticket sales counter was advertising for his "in stores," scheduled sit-ins by local musicians, the most prominent being Baker Faraday, whose name randomly peppered the month of August.

Baker's attention was drawn to the rectangular spaces between the posters, as if a certain point in time was missing. "You know, brother," said B.A. in answer to Baker's inquisitive stare, "I used to have Che, Mao, Karl, Fidel, and the rest plastered all over the store." He got lost in a bit of reverie. "Sometimes it's later than sooner you realize your folly—and burn away as much of that life as possible."

"Better later than never," answered Baker, picking up a 1976 Gran Torino model—red, with a large white vector stripe down each side—from the shelf. "When did you burn them?"

B.A. pointed to the six-foot painting of Jesus Christ over the cash register. "Brother, they all went out when He came in." He made a humble sign of the cross. "No more selling weed and mushrooms out the back door. It's high time—no pun intended, Lord—that I finally bury such a litany of life embarrassments and start earning my ticket to paradise."

Baker walked up to a man gripped in an emotional moment, grabbing and squeezing his shoulders. "Love to hear it, B."

The cheesy décor held the atmosphere in a perpetual time warp of mild chaos. It was genuine and hospitable but at the same time held a faint undertone of importance. The passion for music was unbridled and consequential, a replica of B.A.'s own mindset. His seven-inch-singles aisle was always popular with the serious vinyl-heads. A dedicated section was reserved for local artists and "should be's." There was secondhand and rarities, reissues for the baby boomers. Indie/punk and metal was judiciously kept separate from the folk, jazz, and soul. And B.A. still meticulously sequestered his anthologies, all "Greatest Hits" and "Best of" collections, in the far corner, seen by this store owner as the hangers-on of rehashed reunion tours and "unplugged" recites. "They simply lack the inspiration of originality to be placed front and center," B.A. had said. "But do they sell," he said with a chuckle. "Do they sell."

Albums weren't grouped under the bulk headings of rock and country. Rather, B.A. separated these catchall references by social affiliation, so Gen-Xers knew where to go for R.E.M., U2, and Guns N' Roses; hippies could go directly to the Grateful Dead, Phish, and Umphrey's McGee; and old-school conservatives could bypass pop country if what they wanted was honky-tonk or tribute songs to those who fought for their country.

Next to the power pop and hip-hop, in a rack called "Eurodance/Electronica," Baker found himself flipping through foreign titles, names he'd never heard.

"I know, I know, Bake. This techno stuff is way manu-factured. But the DJs buy this stuff up. It comes over from Europe. It seems I've become the linchpin to the whole dance scene around here. How crazy is that? I mean, this music gets me flat seasick."

Baker picked up a copy of *Lange*. "So this is that wow-wow-whada-wow-sounding stuff, eh?"

"Well, Bake, what you are describing is house music. What you got there is trance. It's more like boom-tick-boom-tick..."

Baker looked to B.A. with a raised eyebrow of concern.

"What, Baker! I gotta know my product. If it comes in plastic, no matter how drastic, dude, to someone it's flippin' fantastic."

B.A.'s best customer looked momentarily to the ceiling. "Did you think of that all by yourself?"

Baker slalomed past the thousands of albums he had flipped through before to get to the back of the store, the sought destination. The lunch hour had brought in several customers, more than the month before, and his face bright-ened to the notion that vinyl might be making a comeback.

Baker saw the bulky, analog nature of the past becoming counterculture to everything music was becoming. But B.A. was doing his part to revive the former institution. An LP evangelist to the day he dies, the stout, dingy man on the corner of Fifteenth and Market would continue to provide the connection between fans and artists. To people like Baker, Cecil, and B.A., the music needed size and presence. The experience of crowding around a record player was communal, leaning in as the lead-in groove broke into the first track. Examining imaginative graphics on a template big enough to reveal the art and perusing liner notes were aspects of personal interaction with the band, something CDs couldn't pull off, unable to supply the emotional connection. Baker could remember playing KISS's *Alive II* so many times that the needle would slide right to the center, unable to hold the diminished groove worn right off the record. But he still had the album. After all, to Baker, it was like a work of art.

The record store contained variety that was second to none. But for those who graced the door of Sleeve and Jacket with regularity, it was behind the beaded curtains where the fresh tunes waited. It was at this doorway B.A. waited with a beaming grin, under thatched hair that looked freshly mussed by his mother, an appearance that resembled a descendent from the loins of Wavy Gravy. And always wearing an apology for a shirt, a remnant from a tour twenty-five years ago, he would waft out an arm, his eyes popping from his head in excitement like olives on a cocktail toothpick.

He parted the way for any enthusiast with a grin of accepted brotherhood, perpetually tagging every greeting with a line of loyal affection. "Welcome to where the prizes lie," he said to Baker, who had already heard this ramble on several occasions. However, Baker would let the line out, allowing his big friend to run with it a while.

B.A. followed Baker inside. Prematurely dropping the beads in Cecil's face as he passed into the dimly lit room, B.A.

turned all attention to who he knew was more than a loyal patron but also the "best freakin' guitar player around!"

Wafting his arms about, B.A. continued. "Today's music scene is drying up tributaries such as this, my friend, leaving the passages damned to no exodus. Soon, only a deep, unintelligible pool of saccharine will remain, uninhabitable to those with a backbone of integrity, leaving us all driven to extinction by the trend of amphibious simplicity." B.A. back-pedaled with a demonstrative row around the room. "But for now, my unmapped creek still contains a bit of white water, crashing currents caused by the truest form of the release, rescued before the mastering houses compress the nuance straight out of the original artform. So hop on my raft and float 'round the analog groove. At least until the digital age sucks us all into their whirling cesspool of the undedicated and musically impaired. Any questions? E-N-J-O-Y."

B.A. was minor league in the big-business sense and wondered how much time he had before his niche became a fond memory, before the internet and dollar downloads blew the remaining few out of the water. But even with his back against the wall, money came second if the opportunity to enlighten someone ever presented itself, especially the youth, who stood on the other side of *his* generation's growing cultural fissure. But B.A. was there to bridge the gap, limbering up his legs to leap across, bringing as many kids back with him as possible, to a place where they might put down the latest Jay-Z release in favor of Eshon Burgundy. Maybe he could cajole them to mix in some Red with their steady dose of Tool, some Decyfer Down with Soundgarden.

B.A. charged a lower price than any record store in town. And haggling was welcome if not expected, for *this* curator's goal was to spread the sound and sew together the divide of dissimilarity that grew wider with each passing year. B.A. pointed to the wall, through the wall, toward his competition. "The neo-hippies and emo kids with momma's money shop at Virgin," he said with a flare of dissonance. And in realizing he had stepped off his moral tract, B.A. breathed in deeply, bringing himself back to center. "These tragic trustafarians have yet to appreciate the satisfaction of finding a good deal." He crossed his arms, puffing out his chest. "I'm here for all the have-less lads. And wait in earnest as the example for the others."

Baker and Cecil shared the room with a boy who could be no older than nineteen, a kid who probably never missed an all-ages show highlighting wall-shaking sequenced sound and parental-advisory lyrics. He had been coming the same day as Baker and Cecil for the last six months, and in his gradual transformation, Baker saw a mutation into a hybrid consumer, a model thrill seeker with a bit of his own persona sewn in. He noticed points of uncanny similarity, the ever-increasing dogmatic quality of searching for inspiration in rows upon rows of new vinyl, not leaving until the last selection was flipped and pondered upon.

Behind the perpetual pissed-off demeanor, the Limp Bizkit T-shirt, and the baggy industrial-strength pants stood a surrogate of Baker's younger days. Baker saw the kind of kid who wouldn't hesitate to paint *DISCO SUCKS* in five-foot letters on a water tower, the kind of kid who calls a radio station just to tell the DJ to pipe down and let the music run its course.

Baker had never spoken to him, only nodded a greeting whenever they momentarily took their eyes off what they'd come to see. But he liked him all the same. He still bought the bands Baker was too old and set in his ways to admire, but he also dug deeper, taking away experimental music in hopes of broadening his taste, for B.A. gave everyone the money-back guarantee, with the opportunity for a trial run on the store headphones. And when Baker noticed the kid had tucked under his arm the only album Blind Faith ever made, he smiled to the notion the kid knew of the band at all. Chosen by one of today's mystified youth, one who, in Baker's eyes, maybe saw a bit clearer than most.

B.A. read off Baker's selections, Bill Bruford, Prince, Dixie Dregs, Rodrigo y Gabriella, and Skillet. He put his hands on the counter and leaned forward as if spreading for the cops, striking the procedural pose he had gotten to know well as a youth. "All over the map, as usual, my man."

Baker could have dipped into his last paycheck, but a few freak summer thunderstorms had kept work to a minimum, though B.A. never minded getting paid by barter, especially when it came to *this* particular guitar player. From behind the counter, B.A. grabbed the mahogany neck of his Fender Custom Telecaster. The blue sunburst around the bridge held the pockmarks of a well-traveled instrument. Yet over the years, the sound still held true. B.A. dropped his head and presented his Special Edition guitar to Baker as if bequeathing the sword of a Templar Knight. "Take her for a spin, my friend."

Baker took his place between two Peavey speaker cabinets, working his fingers for a midday jam. As he twisted the tuning pegs to his liking, B.A. carefully took each of Baker's records out of its sleeve, to check for scratches and to say goodbye to another treasure. And as the sound of one well-used guitar blew out into the Denver afternoon, a hot-dog vendor pushed his cart closer to the door of Sleeve and Jacket, in readiness for a big payday from the crowd that began to gather.

The room had first filled with those familiar with the "in store" calendar. Then the curious peeked in, dipping their toes ever so slightly into the doorway before finding the scene palatable, made safe by the talent sitting in the far-right corner.

Thirty minutes later, Baker could feel no greater high. His emotional energy and array of styles drew in a stout attendance, providing B.A. another opportunity to evangelize upon the masses.

In the heart of downtown, interpretation of the Bible would send people fleeing, insulted by words that so easily got under their skin. The former hippie knew speaking of Christ was an eggshell walk through the minefield of political correctness. But B.A. planned for these impromptu groups, and always owned an uncanny knack of ad-libbing a personal homily.

He knew the approach must be figurative. Reciting scripture would be lost on those who were agnostic at best. It needed a personal touch, so finding a theological current of the day was vital. Baker leaned over his guitar, anxious for what might happen next. For good or bad, he enjoyed this moment especially. For B.A. to turn just one mind toward heaven, even for a split second, made the effort worthwhile. And for anyone whose heart was closed tight to the mystery of faith, the door was always open. Anyone was free to leave. And they often did.

"Thank you for dropping by today to listen to the God-given talents of the mighty Baker Faraday. Now, before you return to the busy world outside my threshold, may I ask that we have your ear for one more?" He turned to Baker. "How about something off *Southern Hospitality?*"

"Track 3, perhaps?" answered Baker in a grateful grin.

"You da' man."

B.A. supplied Baker with a microphone, but over the months, he had yet to use it. A vocalist Baker was not, far too flat and abrasive to allow the comfort he needed to ever open his mouth onstage. His voice would certainly draw away from the guitar, which to him was the star. But he could not deny that there were shades of envy toward those who could carry a tune. He knew all too well that more important to his own ability was the required mouthpiece, both willing and able to spread the Gospel by Baker's side. Nat was the best, but B.A. was a close second.

"Before you exit this place of joy and love, allow me to give you fair warning."

Baker grabbed the crudest guitar tone he could find and began to beat the crowd over the head with a raucous riff. B.A. put one foot far forward, grabbing the microphone in both hands, rocking to the rhythm in his best portrayal of Jack Black.

> *I'm feeling everything's about to blow.*
> *I'm feeling everything's about to blow?*
> *I'm feeling everything's about to blow!*
> *Here He comes, undefeated, undisputed*
> *3-2-1*

Slamming down on the bone-crushing chords, Baker looked up to the crowd, finding the dichotomy in the onlookers who made his purpose so pleasurable. Of the tens in attendance, some who had a clean exit to the door dashed out in horror. Others shared in the motivation to leave, but the majority who remained pressed them forward toward this demonstrative fat man, either maintaining a serious focus on the lyrics or marveling at the complete bombast of Born Again.

> *Relentless earth, coming to collect,*
> *Hidden from the awaited day of rest,*
> *The feet that swell, walk the memories of late,*
> *Wrapped around the heart of a pity masquerade.*

B.A. stepped into the crowd. He approached a young man of college age. He wore his hair long, sideburns flared and well groomed, a shabby-chic look rounded out by an Urban Outfitters T-shirt logoed with a company that didn't exist. He wore a dejected countenance, mouth turned up on one side. His eyes portrayed a mind full of academic indoc- trination, of the Darwinian mold, B.A. surmised. He was a know-it-all, full of one-liners from the bumper-sticker drawer in his mind, a guy smart enough to talk in circles for hours without saying a thing. These were B.A.'s favorite subjects, individuals wrapped up in disapproving pessimism, standing with arms crossed as if looking for an intellectual fight.

Full of the Holy Spirit, the ridiculous saint of Sleeve and Jacket bounced over to get inside the man's comfort zone. The man unwitting of the approaching attention, his eyes wid- ened at such girth and dogged determination as B.A. zoned in. With one big arm now flopping over his shoulder, the subject of B.A.'s attention began to shrink. The tough facade that defined his character was replaced by a meek cast of helplessness. But soon, the thought of being caught in such a ridiculous situation caused a remnant of a smile to flash across the man's face before he playfully pushed B.A. away.

> *The moon has turned to blood,*
> *Baptized in vengeance flame.*
> *They shake at what's to come*
> *When He breaks the seals of pain.*

B.A. bounced around the room, out of body, as his frizzled hair swung manically, whipping across his face.

> *So roll back the prison bars,*
> *For charity, not fame,*
> *Till the streets will over run*
> *With the tongues that shout the name.*

A woman in lawyerly attire ducked away, not put off by the entertainment, just aghast to share in the sweat that now dripped from B.A.'s brow.

> *Watch out,*
> *Get down now,*
> *No doubt,*
> *321,*
> *I'm feeling everything's about to blow ...*

Several in the crowd raised "rock on" finger signs. B.A. stroked down on his shadow guitar in synchronicity to Baker's notes. The song ended with an ovation that spun heads around out on the sidewalk. As the cheers died down, another opportunity to leave presented itself. But no one moved. Such an event in the middle of Wednesday was odd, and newcomers would stretch their lunch hour a bit more, waiting to see if it was over.

B.A. wiped a towel over his mouth. His eyes panned a crowd much younger than he. His antics had trimmed the fat, paring down the gathering to those willing to witness the next step in B.A.'s spiritual manifest. Some he knew from church. Some he only knew by their presentation, those who owned faces at rest that he easily ascertained carried either the contentment provided by a relationship with Christ or the grief-stricken, downcast expression of one coveting contempt over love.

He paused a moment and then laughed hysterically. It came out unexpectedly, like a sneeze, and it was contagious, causing a roll of chuckles that widened outward like a ripple on water. "I have something to show you all," B.A. said and produced an old, worn trench coat as if out of thin air. It was a deep, dark blue, longer than a modern style, and worn on the elbows. In one arm of the coat was what appeared to be a bullet hole. Three other similar holes could also be seen. The shoulders appeared somewhat darker, as if they had one day adorned military-style epaulets.

B.A. slipped it on. "I have a new coat," he said.

The obvious condition of the coat made the statement seem ridiculous, and laughter rose again in the room.

B.A. was undaunted. He held out his arms, displaying the garment further.

"It was designed by God and given to me by Jesus Christ. All I had to do to receive this coat was to believe in God's only Son." He began walking the room. "I find it fits me perfectly unless I allow myself to become puffed up with foolish pride—then it's too tight. If I walk with my head high, trying to be above those about, then it is too short. But if I walk humbly, as I should before God, it fits me just right."

He pointed out to a crowd grown silent. "How is the coat made, you may ask? The shoulders are wide and roomy so that I can help my fellow man carry his burdens."

B.A. approached each spectator closest to him, looking them in the eye with reverent sincerity. "The collar is made of God's mercy. Yes, the mercy of God's promises. First that I may become his child, and second that I will one day dwell with Him in that home prepared for His saints. The cuffs are narrow so that there is no room to tuck away grievance and hard feelings toward my neighbors."

"The pockets are oversized," B.A. continued. With a thumb, he spread the mouth of each hip pocket open, and inside, to the bystander, it was surprisingly dark, bottomless. "One is for the love of God. The other is to hold my love for my fellow man . . . and all humanity."

He paced on in a circle, close enough to the crowd that they may get a close look. Some felt an otherworldly draw to his coat and were moved to touch it.

"There are three buttons on my coat, which stand for faith, hope, and charity. I check on them often so that none becomes loose or lost."

He splayed the coat open. "The lining is made of God's forgiveness, which I need so often that I want it next to me at all times."

Closing it again, B.A. cinched the coat, pulling the straps through the front buckle, never peering down at the task, effortless. "The belt is made of God's love that encircles me every day. The material is thick enough to protect me when the storms of life come my way but not so thick that I will not be able to feel the presence of the Holy Spirit who guides me. There are many threads in my new coat but not one thread of doubt that God's promises are true."

Again B.A. chose a person in the crowd he did not recognize. One hand on her cheek, she wore a look of incredulity, as if a warmth she had not sensed before welled inside her chest. B.A. looked at her with deep sympathetic eyes, giving her the impression that they were alone, conveying to her that she was special. "Do you wonder about the color of my coat? Why, it's the color of Jesus's eyes that must sparkle when a lost soul accepts Him."

She appeared to want to cry. Reaching out, she put her hand on his outstretched arm, touching the sleeve. And B.A. held her hand there for just a moment, enough time for the energy of the Lord to move her. A glimmer creased her eyes, and a single tear fell down her face.

"I will need my coat all through life. When I travel through the valley of death and when I view the future, I will always wear my new coat."[2]

B.A. paused, holding his fist to his mouth, the shoulders of such a robust man rising as he stifled his own emotions. A few tender moments passed before he spoke again. "All of you, thanks for coming . . . and thanks for staying."

---

[2] The "My Jacket" sermon is not mine, but I am unable to find the person who wrote it. I just found it to be beautiful.

Born Again's untamed sermons lifted Baker to heights of profound reflection. He had told his friend as much. But B.A. would scoff at the accolade, for any personal achievement is secondary to the feeling of being chosen by God as the vessel to spread the Good News. He had been saved, and any brief talents lent out to him by the Lord were humbly accepted. "To reach a level as to touch even one wandering soul is a glorious attainment," he would say. "These blessings are to taste the sweetest berries off the vine."

Regaining his jollity, Born Again reached for Baker, bringing him over to his side. "Remember, my friends . . ." He cast a gaze toward Mr. Sideburns. "However gloomy may become your outlook, the uplook is glorious."

Cecil sat on a two-stack of milk crates, close to Baker, as a groupie does. The sermon had sparked a flood of thoughts. He pulled out a small pad with contorted spirals from his shirt pocket. He clicked a pen against his chest and scribbled with speed and without a pause, for a profound poet Cecil was, finding inspiration in the smallest events, which would often throw him into a dream state where the ink flew as if on autopilot.

As with many poets, attempts were made that fell short, ending in a collection of wadded-up paper at the bottom of the desk-side receptacle. But Cecil's poetry was spot-on, always, as these were messages pushed by the Holy Spirit to identify the moment at hand and conceptualize its meaning. This episode was no different. In fact, it was more enlightening than any recent revelry he could recall.

It was a short poem, meant for Baker, not now but in time, in the near future. In the words, he saw a purpose, a possible remedy to a future of pain. A test was at hand, and Cecil looked to the ceiling, through it, to the sky above, and nodded in acceptance to the challenges that lay ahead.

Cecil looked at Born Again as he placed his prop with care over the counter. *So many pockets*, Cecil thought as he made his way over for a closer look.

7

IN DEEP DARKNESS, THERE SHINES A LIGHT

Lorenzo walked along the earth's cool tropical floor embellished in organic aquamarine, with ornaments of red-pink teardrop petals and the hibiscus shedding saffron pollen like confetti as his legs whisked by. He took deep breaths, inhaling fresh scents of ambrosia, an effluvium of floral fragrances that danced around his nose in a gypsy waft. As he walked in nothing but a loincloth, his skin felt moist and soft, like a newborn carried in the balmy sea breeze.

Lorenzo could hear the ocean in the distance, the sound thrown off as it ricocheted through the dense foliage. But his direction was exact nonetheless, drawn by the desire to be held aloft by the sea, cared for in its enormity, just as he remembered.

Lorenzo could see boughs of light as they penetrated the dim tranquility of the tree canopy, hitting the ground like tiny spotlights on a mini-scopic world. Charmed by the flicker in the beams, he put a hand out to catch it, to feel its warmth. But when Lorenzo's palm met the beam, the light struck him with the surprise of searing pain, shooting through his body as a blazing meteor tears through space.

Breathing in the odor of burning flesh, Lorenzo bellowed out. It took everything he had to pull free of the sensation, a shot of pain that coursed his body as if a spike had been driven through. But as Lorenzo moved forward, another dose of fire struck him in his side, dropping him to his knees, into a roll as his body coiled into a protective ball on the ground.

He writhed upon a bed of palm fronds as they sliced into his skin like razor blades. His teeth clenched together in a vice as his mind flashed senseless in the anguish of his pain, seeing only snippets of malignant visions from his childhood between the split-second strobes of blinding white light. In search of strength, Lorenzo reached deeper in his mind, blocking out these injections of agony in hopes of finding a way out. And it was there, in the farthest recess of memory, where he found Lincoln, glowing in the aura of the Almighty. Through his grit, Lorenzo uttered two words that dribbled weakly from his mouth. "H-e-l-p M-e-e-e-e."

As if time and space had been folded, Lorenzo found himself gagging on salt water from the tide that brushed the shore over his supine body. He pushed himself off the smooth water-swept sand, backing off a few steps before getting his feet under him once again. Lorenzo's dilated eyes blinked ceaselessly in the penetrating luminescence of the sun. He groped his body for wounds but found none. Then, as he lifted his head, his gaze came to focus upon a solitary sandbar one hundred yards out into the sea. Something impelled him, maybe it was an escape, a place where the torturous wrath couldn't reach him. Without a second thought, he treaded out into the water, toward the perceived safe haven of his recollection, as the repetitive tide erased each footprint in his wake.

Weakened from the distress of unbelievable events, Lorenzo crawled up onto the hump of sand with his last gasp of energy. And when he raised his head in small triumph, what he saw, he could not believe.

A man stood before him. Lorenzo noticed the golden Rasta lion hanging from his neck, and he collapsed under the heavy emotion of seeing Lincoln again, standing resolute in the afterlife of youth. Lorenzo was too consumed in his own fatigue to speak, but Lincoln's words prompted his mind to find a center, the eye of the storm between his nervous exhaustion and physical grief.

"Get'tup, young Zo."

The intonation of Lincoln's voice rang like clanging cathedral bells through the chambers of his soul. As Lorenzo ascended to his knees, and then to his feet, he met the eyes of Lincoln's ghost, and a wash of shame flooded over his body for what he had become after his mentor's passing. He looked for some form of apology, but it was a search in vain, knowing of nothing that he could say to justify the life he had led.

As tears welled up in his bloodshot eyes, Lorenzo looked to his omnipotent cleric, a man he was so lucky to have had as his paternal guide. But Lorenzo saw in Lincoln's bright but stoic glare that their meet held no bliss of a family reunion, knowing there would be no embrace over time lost, for Lincoln's face held no evidence of mercy as he raised his hands out from his sides.

"Step inna di ring of them da'kest fears, young warrior."

As Lorenzo followed the line of Lincoln's long, drifting finger, somehow he knew what loomed at the end. He felt his heart grow heavy under the ponderous thought of what would happen next. But regardless of his fear, Lorenzo understood his duty, putting one foot in, then the other, careful not to disturb the arc of this familiar circle of battle.

Once he was inside, his fists clenched, his head raced, not wanting to take his eyes from Lincoln's beautiful face, not wanting to look at who now joined him. But once the Rastafarian's attention turned to the one opposing Lorenzo, he had no choice but to confront his own fate or forever live under the unknown consequence of his most tragic mistake.

The one who stood before him was naked, faceless, bleeding rivulets of blood from the same areas that wounded Lorenzo before. His shoulder bulged with the same branded gang insignia Lorenzo wore on his. Though, in addition, he wore tattoos of hate and violence over so much of his body that a patch of untouched white skin was almost nonexistent. And Lorenzo recognized each and every one. Malik had worn the power markings of a gang leader, on epaulets signifying criminal achievements. Harold preferred knives dripping red. The Magnum, the Glock, and the AR-15 belonged to Cyrus.

But worse than bringing to light the memory of these former leaders of the Shade was the one mark that stood out over this being's heart; surrounded by these ominous symbols of death and destruction was the name of his love, *NINA*.

"*Yuh 'ave dee'fined yor'self by de bullet,*" said Lincoln in a deep resounding bellow, a speech void of any mortal quality. "*And fah'dis yuh dwell inna de pity of yuh own undoing.*"

Once again, Lorenzo could not hold back his anguish, and as he dropped to his knees in penitence, tears dropped from his cheeks, fusing with the pools of blood formed by the manifestation that loomed over him.

"What can I do?" asked Lorenzo, through the cracks in the fingers that held his face in disgrace.

"*Yuh 'ave chanted the mantra of luv an' hate an fah'dis yuh soul resides inna limbo. Luk to yuh heart, young Zo. De innocent is alive but bleeds ah riva of dis'con'tent. But by blessings him has been saved. Find him an' share inna de Glory of Jah.*"

Lorenzo looked up through his watering eyes. "He's alive?"

"*Give thanks and praise, Zo. De bane of yuh existence walks dis earth. It nuh longa ah time of regret but ah time for re'birt. It be'up to yuh, young Zo. Mi can see nuh furda.*"

The ground broke, sand heaved, and Lorenzo fell through the blackness between sleep and consciousness. When he opened his eyes, it was a new day, with Aaron watching over him, a curious twist in his expression. "Suh how him, Lorenzo. How is mi old bredren . . . Lincoln?"

Seven days later, Nina sat in the sand, hugging her knees tight to her chest. It was now the eighth day since Lorenzo had been taken into Aaron's care. *It is taking too long*, she said, softly to the Lord, as if He sat with her, as she knew He did—pleased, Nina hoped, that she was learning to pray, to confide in Him.

Nina had a week in solitude, living a monastic life as she authored her words up to God, tapering her thoughts through meditation to be less random, more sincere, as she would speak to a friend. Nina's prayers had become sound, pulling from the deepest regions of her heart and mind. Her determined pleas to her Lord and Savior became a conversation throughout the day and night as she ascended in power and confidence, knowing she would never be alone again.

Nina had improved her reading by a single book, and she enhanced her knowledge of God by the Bible. The pages between the leather were ancient but timeless. And Aaron showed her how to travel the Book, not to start at page one but to move around the text of the Old Testament, finding the stories that made the most sense.

But Aaron's was a Hebrew Bible. And when she left his care, she was given a text of the same to help her grow in devout strength. With Aaron, the story was so much clearer, able to draw down to a concise translation any passage too unnatural for Nina to grasp. Now, alone with the words, the Book was a challenge. The strings of genealogies, the strange laws, left her perplexed. But it was reading the prophecies that led her to childhood memories, of Christmas, the birth of Jesus Christ.

It was God she knew in the persona of a man, a man who died for her sins, she was told, by her mother aside a Christmas tree. Nina was cradled in her lap, against her bosom, under arms that held Nina so tight, in simple, beautiful moments, before she gave up on dignity and gave in to her poverty, before self-pity took hold and love was lost.

What little her mother had bestowed on Nina, she had planted one vital seed at an impressionable time. It lay dormant for years, but the contour made by the single annual story had remained through the highs and lows of youth, creating the extents of her experience, of what would become her spiritual life.

It was to be the New Testament that energized her journey. In her perusals, she learned of the unyielding faith of the apostles, the enduring love shown in the face of evil, His parables, His passion.

Read, pray, repeat. *Don't forget to eat something, stay hydrated.*

Her days would be perceived as the height of uselessness by anyone she knew. But Nina knew no one, not really—only Lorenzo, or who she hoped with all her heart he could be again. All she had was time, and she would use this time to transcend above her bleak surroundings in wait for the other half of her life to return.

She held her eyes closed, her pupils moving back and forth as she dropped into deep ruminations, reflecting upon her short time with Aaron, recalling the words that allayed her suffering.

I am part of an imperfect world, but I am no longer broken. My enemy created in me virtue. Within my fate, I was shown mercy. But the evil was welcomed, and for this, I am an addict. My addiction is a guest in my house, but I will not allow it a seat at my table.

It is malignant and deathless, but God is my protector. Through Him, with Him, and in Him, I will walk the axis and not falter.

Fully absorbed in her deliberations, she did not hear the footfalls on the sand. And when she opened her eyes, she saw a transformation. Lorenzo glowed at the sight of his beautiful Nina. He bent down, touched her hair gently, felt the soft skin under her chin. Nina took his hands, kissing them, as tears of joy rolled down her cheeks.

Lorenzo held her face, lightly brushing away the tear trails with his thumbs. Their faces were only inches apart, eyes fixed on each other. Lorenzo's breath felt labored, as if running from something, to something he hoped was still there. "Tell me, Nina . . . what have I lost?"

Nina rose to her feet, not relinquishing the hold she had on Lorenzo's hands, tilting her head, her shoulders raised ever so slightly. "Tell me a memory, Lorenzo."

A memory, so many impressions on his mind and soul, once as significant as flesh and blood, had become nearly inaudible echoes, faded shadows of an early evening as everything Lorenzo used to love had turned. But eight days later,

Lorenzo's blurred illusions began to take shape, and over the last two days, he had bounced all that had been wonderful off Aaron, who sat patiently, knowing each recollection was a stair step out of darkness.

One memory became two, and two became a chronology of each profound event of their short lives together. But only the good times were brought to light, for the bad were recent; they were fresh and familiar wounds that needed to stay under a mindful gauze until each was strong enough again.

Lorenzo spoke at times with his eyes closed, visualizing pure days of youth, bringing up moments Nina had forgotten. His recollection of their relationship was lucid, thoughtful, and only about Nina, the things she had said, her expressions, every minute mannerism Nina could never realize—only Lorenzo, the boy who fell in love the moment she walked into his life.

By the time Lorenzo was finished, the night had bled away the day, and they sat together under the brilliant stars of a new-moon night. He took her hands once again. "I'm back, Nina. I'm at your side . . . and I'll never leave it. I'd like to think what we have been through . . ." He paused. "What I put'choo through can bring us closer."

Lorenzo never took his eyes off Nina's, almost having a look of urgency, a childlike excitement that may have seemed out of place. Only Nina knew of what Lorenzo meant, of what Aaron had taught them both. "We found God, Nina, or God found us."

Nina took her love in a lasting embrace, her head upon his chest. "He has always been with us, baby. But by the gift he bestowed upon us, the gift of free will, to choose good or evil, we were tempted away from Him. And for this, we were bound in chains." Nina pushed back to meet Lorenzo's eyes again. "But He sent us Aaron. He sent us Lincoln."

Lorenzo's hands gripped Nina's elbows. "You saw Lincoln?"

Nina looked out over the sands. "Not exactly. I mean, I felt him. I felt him often, as if he was always close by. And you? Did you feel him?"

Lorenzo's face tightened, recalling his inscrutable pose, his passive but sober expression. "You could say that."

The dream had opened a door, and the light was so divine he nearly broke down again. But instead, he smiled his smile, bigger than ever, realizing he now had the strength to tell Nina everything, or almost everything.

Once the space had been swept out of tinfoil, aluminum cans, straws, and broken glass, the crack den of the village became a reliable space to practice in. In an environment dripping in horrible memories, the space presented a duplicity that was difficult to ignore. But the challenge would be met square on, together. There was no veil to throw over what the boys had been through. No temptations of returning to that life would be suppressed. The five of them represented a spontaneous support group.

Without a counsellor, a veteran of the habit who might possess the right words at the right time, it would be Lorenzo to take on the burden of leadership. He had possessed the capacity to lead the gang into hell. Now it was his burden to bring his boys into the light.

Lorenzo used the ruin of the environment to their advantage. The unkempt sanctum of drug use offered them the opportunity to get down to work, giving each of them something to do, knowing idle time presented a static target for their demons. But the room also carried ghosts of a recent past, dark romanticisms of the deadly sins that still stalked the hall. It would be the transformation of the physical condition that would chase away their recollection of calamity. Being absorbed in the purpose pushed back skeptical thoughts of failure. The space would soon be complete, the melancholy waned, as the sweetness of the tropical breeze blew in the front windows and the chemical scents of puppet lives blew out the back.

Nina did not partake in the toils of the day. Rather, she would take deliberate observation of young men doing the thing the men needed to do. And to her satisfaction, their eyes did not hold the fearful look of wanton need. Rather, it was the expression she looked for, she prayed for, to lose that appearance of demoralizing anxiety, feeling life would now go on without the disease to fall back on.

The five were reawakened, and they were locked into a newfound look of astute confidence. One by one, Aaron had taken them in. And one by one, they returned, to begin their own pilgrimage under the protection their newfound faith had given them. Nina had carried the torch into the unknown,

creating a confidence in Lorenzo and the others that if aspira-
tion could get out ahead of need, a new authority may emerge.
By Nina's, and then Lorenzo's, appeal, boys known as Sketchy,
Flu, Viper, and Ratman entered Aaron's domain. But they
were to go no further, not until the gang tag was dropped.
And from that day, they would again be known as Luther,
Cassius, Booker, and Amos, the names given to them at birth.

Under his charge, Aaron found that each of these boys
not only had never been loved but had never known love.
They reacted so well to being cared for, to being given attention around the clock, caressed, spoken to with kindness,
gentleness. As their minds grew in clarity, they found the
love of perfect strangers to be the greatest joy. For the sin-
gular attention of another, the boys embraced the company
of the elders as parents and grandparents they wished they
had, should have had.

As night fell, practice commenced in the living room.
Nina stayed in the adjoining room, separated from them by
damaged drywall over wood studs, not wanting her imprint
cast on what they needed to do as brothers. In the dim, she
pulled out a chair, smoothed her denim skirt, and composed
herself before taking the same seat as so many junkies had
before. Candles were affixed to the tables within their own
settled wax, always off center, as they were pulled toward the
addict that required the heat, until it was established in front
of someone whose chair could have been engraved, reserved
through familiarity with a personal flame, a light that never
let the abuser down.

Nina lit the stump that was left of the candle. She watched the flame dance, and suddenly, but not unexpectedly, the craving presented itself. From hiding out in the back of Nina's psyche, the addiction felt invited to walk through the doorway, to take the opportunity to entice a weakened state. Nina watched the fire bow and wave for her to come forward. She felt safe as the fire spoke, using Nina's voice within her head. The voice attempted to reconnect Nina to her habit, to reattach her synapse network in favor of the enemy's desires.

She gave her demon the opportunity. It was purposeful, for Nina did not want to look over her shoulder any longer, in worry about the next time she would be tempted. Rather, Nina lit the candle, boldly luring her adversary. But such an audacious act would not transpire before prayer, not before building her strength, hammering out her shield, her sword. And through the endowment received from Jesus Christ, Nina was equal to the task.

I will not give in to you. You are a shifting shadow. My god is unfailing in goodness and love, a beacon of light in the darkness. He has bestowed upon me the gift of endurance. I will always outlast you, extinguish anything you force upon me. There is no longer anything you can offer.

Nina leaned in toward the flame. And as if it knew this trial would bear no fruit, it stood stoic, upright, ready for Nina to blow it out.

She watched the smoke ascend, dissipate, and disappear. Nina brought her hands up, wafting it to her face. The outflow of the extinguished candle brought a tangible essence that struck her emotionally. And Nina felt purified, as if the angels of heaven took up the nefarious spirit and freed Nina's soul.

Within such a profound and holy moment, Nina closed her eyes to better hear.

The music ascended above mediocrity, much to her delight, as Nina never missed a practice, serving as devoted lookout for Cyrus's return. Such secrecy continued for some time, long enough for a party of feds on taxpayer Harleys to get into the flow of the general's dealings. Malik would be rolling in his grave to see his personally trained officer in shackles, pressed up against the brick wall of Sloppy Joe's Bar. Cyrus was sentenced to the stature of many he had supplied, to suffer through the monotony of incarceration and Aramark bologna dinners offered up in so many foul ways, within the walls of the Chattahoochee pen for the next four to ten.

Little was Lorenzo's concern that he was next in line to take over the Shade. Realizing the chaos that had developed in the ranks, he allowed the formidable gang to vaporize as easily as the heroin under a low flame. Malik rolled once again, while Lincoln chortled.

With Cyrus in chains, by default, Lorenzo had another fine instrument bequeathed to his keeping. And without the intimidating onus of their former general hanging over them, the five young men could now freely call themselves "Everlivin'." After what constituted bygone lives, they felt sustained in their circadian survival over the beast, almost immortal, less concerned with matters not linked to their personal religion.

> *Trust no future, however pleasant,*
> *Let the dead past bury its dead;*
> *Act, act in the living present,*
> *Heart within, and God overhead.*[3]

Though they played reggae, the five failed to bond with the politics of Rastafari. Beyond the muddle of drug use and the malaise of those confined to the village, they realized opportunity had always been there for the taking. It was discovered that the sense of Babylon was an embedded philosophy, embraced by Down on Uptown as the greatest aspect to take away. But as Lorenzo reflected on his young life, the only ones to ever hold him back were the inhabitants of his village. Lorenzo could now clearly see that it was a crutch, an excuse to be pulled out for every shortcoming. To seize upon a self-perpetuated disadvantage was the true slavery, and Lorenzo felt shame for being duped to perceive his work at the guesthouse to be other than what it was, a damn good job.

He looked down the two-lane stretch of asphalt in the direction he had pedaled so many mornings, remembering what was the happiest period of his life. In the simplest terms, he gave an honest day of work and received an honest day's pay, in the beginning. But Lorenzo was tugged at incessantly by his peers, whom he could now see as what they were, the backward state of his small so-called civilization. How punk

---

3 "A Psalm of Life," Henry Wadsworth Longfellow, 1838.

it was to integrate, he had been scolded, chastised, for doing as he was told. He'd been told he was oppressed—by his brothers, his true oppressors—and called ignorant for his cooperation, his deference to the other side of town. But through Aaron's tutelage over a period of eight days, Lorenzo had learned that the minute he stepped into the Shade, he took on the pose of the obtuse cooperator, to satisfy his adolescent need to belong, joining in the fray of disordered selfish desire, void of any semblance of virtue.

Now it was the simplicity he craved again. Lorenzo had realized the hard way that humility is to be the noblest aspect of life well lived.

"Inna di realm of passive resignation, dere is luv, and hate wi' find no purchase tuh manifest."

He would return to Aunt Bea's doorstep, with a metaphysical hat in hand, and apologize for each evil act, itemized in his mind like a tax collector of old. He would offer to work off the trouble he had caused. But Aunt Bea would only take him in her arms, hugging him tight, to release him on his way as she dabbed at her crying eyes, knowing the child had become a man.

The band felt ready to leave their practice space. Within a prayer circle, Lorenzo passionately declared to the members of Everlivin' that everything is attainable, that they were beholden to no one but their Lord and Savior. "Keep sorrow and shame behind you, the purpose to the front."

Nina stood near the window, looking out with her mind, not her eyes. "Out there, events of the woken world will be poured upon you." Walking over to the boys, she curled her arm around Lorenzo's waist. Her face, always so calm and beautiful, mesmerized the young group. She had their utmost attention. "Luther ... Cassius ... Booker ... Amos. Don't give in to illusions. Stay together, keep each other safe, keep the momentum moving forward. Remember ... your treasure is in your harmony for one another." Nina slowly paced, circling the boys, pointing back to the window. "Out there, no one will know of what you have been through."

Draping her arms over Luther and Cassius, she bowed her head, and the others bowed in tandem. "Dear Lord, you know of our spiritual hunger and our quest for greater meaning. Give us the wisdom to know true north in the fog." Nina removed her arms from their shoulders. Entering their circle, she pressed her hands together. "And one more thing, Heavenly Father, it is my prayer to each of these young men that the proper woman will find their grace so appealing that they will be loved in the spirit of Christ, that they will, one day soon, marry in a great celebration."

"That my kids will be blessed with a mother and a father," added Luther.

Cassius said, "That they will go to school."

Booker added, "And they will obey the law."

Amos said, "This is to be our legacy."

"In the name of Jesus, Amen."

As the principal connection of the Shade's drug market, Lorenzo had become a familiar face on Duval and Truman Avenue. At the height of his dealing, Lorenzo stayed disciplined to never impose his operation on the inside of another man's place of business, for this would draw too much attention. Rather, Lorenzo preferred to abide far enough away, down alleys, in parking lots. After all, they all knew where to find him. When proprietors did beckon for Lorenzo's services, he had provided them what they needed at cost, buying their loyalty, thinking he might need a favor someday. And a grateful rejoinder came by way of gigs for his new band, as Everlivin' promptly landed regular spots on the main drag, with weekly visits to Calabash as the house band.

But Lorenzo did not see this as a payback for favorable treatment within the drug trade. They had been invited into a bar scene torn asunder by the hand of the Shade. Unbeknownst to the management, now lost themselves under the haze of addiction, Everlivin' would present themselves as the saviors to any and all who would heed their message. They would dive into the very hell where they had pulled themselves out of only months before, inviting the enemy, not running from it, to save anyone who desired an exit from their habit. For a few hours a night, they would turn the bar into a church, offering service to others as the only way to continue their quest toward the fullest revival of their souls.

In no time, Calabash was packed to see one of the most unique acts in town. Everlivin' had cornered the market in a place too far off the beaten trail for more competent groups. Thus, competition merely consisted of local splinter projects Lorenzo called "spirit chasers," posers who maintained a far lesser pride in their community, those who played Jimmy Buffet covers to the beckoning of the vacationers, tunes so many lifetime locals grew to loathe. And such an indigenous majority ran to see Everlivin', to yell "Amen" at the top of their lungs as a means to cleanse their ears, and minds.

Small-time stardom came easily indeed. And with such good fortune came a growing devotion for one another, forming a coherent support group of best friends with stature enough to provoke the demise of their dark habit. Minds reopened like a creaking door, never to slam shut again. The therapy of the music had saved them, playing with the flaws of new beginnings but joyous toward what they heard just the same.

Reggae music washed over a crowd that gelled in the positive atmosphere of Calabash on Saturday night. Set breaks became sermons as Lorenzo poured out his experience, offering salvation to any and all owning enough wherewithal to try to live again. And one by one, the afflicted would come to Lorenzo, to Nina, gaunt and squalid, existing within husks of their former selves. Some had been customers of the Shade, people Lorenzo knew, though on a very superficial level, as nothing was more phony than the dialogue between the conveyor and the user.

After each show, Lorenzo, Nina, and the band would sit with men and women on the brink of death, to hear their stories, their pleas for their own deliverance. And those who carried the will to choose a better path were sent to Aaron, who for the first time since leaving the village opened his own domain to those who had stolen away his former life. The mottled souls who forced Aaron and his tribe to find refuge would be welcomed. The bitterness for those who destroyed their way of life were taken in with generosity, for Aaron and his clan had found a profound appreciation for the love and care they gave, and it became an addiction unto itself.

Within the environment Everlivin' created, the manifestation of darker impulses seemed to become diffused. The crowd seemed to grab a frequency of unconscious energy through a performance that was hardly sublime. It was why they knew the proclivity of the town to be drawn to their performances, which was divinely inspired. In some way, false principles in the order of selfishness became unsettled through an affectionate regard from the musicians onstage. The passive sentiment from those who many knew as vicious gangbangers provided an inquisitive countermeasure against a neighborhood decline into nihilism. If they could change, well . . .

Indeed. It wasn't the music so much as the vibe. Everlivin' was the big tent revival for the inward longings of the heart. Under the tent was a place void of acrimony, chaos, of lives in reverse. Everlivin' was showing there was an off ramp to anyone's track that was found to be painfully meandering, with all exits leading to spiritual healing.

The dance floor jammed in wait for the next song. Lorenzo circled from behind his kit and approached Luther's microphone. "I'd like to announce a very special guest to the stage for the next number." Lorenzo shaded his eyes and looked out over the crowd. "Nina, baby, would you please join me and the fellas?"

From a back table, Nina put her hand to her chest, eyes moistening, alight in surprise. As she approached, the kindhearted crowd parted the way. Lorenzo took her by the hand as, with a small step forward, she ascended the stage. They held one another in a long embrace before Lorenzo released her, giving Nina a sweet kiss of gratitude and love.

Cassius started into the saintly keyboard hymn. Nina swayed side to side as if in a dream before imparting the lyrics that hit so close to home. Her ethereal voice portrayed "Many Rivers to Cross" in a rare version of womanhood, which sent out the message in a flowing force of clarity. Lorenzo played a simple accompaniment, noticing the faces of a struck audience as they watched his beloved with fixed emotion.

Once an addict, always an addict, they say. But the music brought Lorenzo ever closer to destroying the evil that had concocted his cravings. His drumsticks would sword fight with the demon's steel spoon, knocking him back due to superior reach. But the cook would always be there, waiting for another crack at the title. Though, so would Nina, providing the more favorable edge of two against one.

Nina and Lorenzo made up for time lost during a period when months had gone by like minutes under the influence. The entire ensemble of Everlivin' hung tight as well, enjoying afternoon swims out to ocean sandbars, which peeked out over the tide like the hump of an enormous white whale. For the five members of Everlivin', there was no place better to meet and talk of their roles as young black men and make plans for the days ahead.

It was a cloudless day upon the back of another motionless leviathan where the survivors confessed to what they had known all along. For four members of Everlivin', what they knew to be fact was that Lorenzo had saved their lives and their appreciation could only be repaid with the truth.

"Zo, you ever think about followin' yo' dream?"

"What dreams'at, Luther?"

"Shoo, you know damn well what I'm sayin.'"

Luther looked out to sea. He was closest to Lorenzo and had been picked by the others to set him free. Lorenzo only waited. His jaw muscle clenched with concern as his friend got up another dose of nerve.

"We've all decided it's time ta send you off, ta find yo'self some fine musicians and make it big. Not like no Rasta group, mo' like Miles Davis, or funkier maybe, like Fishbone awe somethin.'"

Unprepared for such a statement, Lorenzo drew a crooked brow at his lead singer. "You betta tell me what you're gettin' at in a damn hurry."

Luther grabbed Lorenzo's shoulder in a means to help his best friend see things more clearly. "Look to yo' future, my brutha. You've got more ability dan all'a us put together an then some. You da one that needs to fly, Zo."

Luther, formerly Sketchy, looked to Cassius, formerly Flu, who had his head down to the sand, where a blowhole would be. He could feel the heat of Luther's eyes on him, beckoning an aid to his opinion.

Without looking up, Cassius spilled out his feelings, the bottom line to the reasoning. "You brought us back, Zo, back from awe graves. We were nothin' until you shined on us, man. It would be a damn injustice to let'choo stay here. Da only way we can repay you is to kick you out. If you stay, it would be on all our con'shen'ses till the day we really *do* cash it in."

Lorenzo was muted by the prospect, the fear of leaving all he knew, when Booker broke the silence. "Nina is a fine woman, Zo. All she talks 'bout is movin' on. Nobody can blame her. She saved you just like you saved us. And now it's time fo' you to come correct. You gotta do right by Nina, Zo."

For the first time in years, Lorenzo was lost in his own defense. And after a moment of the most uncomfortable quiet, he began to dream out loud. "Man. What's out there, fellas? I mean, what's really out there?"

"Whatever's out there," Amos replied, "dis will always be here."

Lorenzo looked over the group with one tear trailing down the side of his hardened youthful face. Luther rose to wipe the sand from his butt and pump up his confused friend.

"Don't even think we're quittin' what we stawted. Shi, we'll find somebody that can hold a reggae beat in no time. Now go find Nina and tell her yer gonna fulfill her every wish, fool."

And one by one, the members of Everlivin' gave Lorenzo the most heartfelt embrace before making their way for the mainland, leaving Lorenzo alone to think it over.

The band had made a pittance compared to their previous illegal endeavors. And with the spending habits they had maintained, Nina and Lorenzo were left with barely enough to get out of town.

It was Nina's decision where they would go. She pondered the map ingrained in her mind to run over all the possibilities. And with smile brimming, she asked Lorenzo how he felt about Colorado; after all, she had always mulled over the thought of fourteen thousand feet into the sky.

The Mustang was filled with only the bare essentials save for one Taylor acoustic guitar that Lorenzo had never so much as strummed. The drum set was left to Everlivin'; the steel drum, however, was put into the care of young Jamal, who gleamed with rapture at the prize.

"Think of me, young brutha."

Jamal grabbed Lorenzo tight around his waist. Lorenzo stroked the boy's head as the lump in his throat grew unbearably large.

Seagulls perched atop streetlights, chests out like sentries overseeing the way in and out. Lorenzo felt their expressionless eyes on him as he drove along the Seven Mile Bridge, impassive, without a presentation of a good omen or a bad, and it gave Lorenzo butterflies in his gut. He looked in the rearview mirror, as if to see asphalt falling away behind him into the sea, disabling any thought of turning back.

No longer would there be the security of the village to fall back on like the arbitrary excuse it had always been. And never would their history be readily known to any new acquaintance. Nina was all that remained of who he was. But who better, he knew, to be by his side than the warrior princess he had known for as long as he knew anything. He looked over to Nina, catching her final entranced glare out on the water. At eighteen, they had lived a lifetime, and this long bridge linking to their home was the umbilical to the all-inclusive, encompassing everything in total. But with each mile, their severed ties drifted farther apart, until the mainland and rebirth into a bigger world.

Lorenzo's eyes remained fixated on the lines of the road as he drove on subconscious autopilot, pondering, as the weight of personal effects in his trunk was nothing compared to the weight he now carried in his mind. Such wrongdoing to humanity over the three years of his addiction was piled so high that he feared he would never be able to come out from under it. It was the worst part about coming clean, remembering the horrific deeds—posing as evil incarnate, selling death to the weak, denouncing all that was pure around him. But one event, one major mistake made a few years ago, sat on his mind as a larger burden than all else combined.

He and "Sketchy" had scoured the neighborhood outside the village, looking for car stereos. It was a hobby of theirs taken up when they didn't have any dealings, when so far under the influence that nothing mattered.

During these crime sprees, these detachments from being, Lorenzo was fearless. He could walk through fire, and if anyone got in his way, he was ready to take care of the situation by any means necessary. And on one stormy night, a night when a rain-soaked Sketchy kept calling into a truck, nagging Lorenzo to hurry it up, one ill-fated man got in his path.

Sketchy was ready to leave the hi-fi and book, knowing no white man could catch them sprinting off on so much coke. But at that time in his life, Lorenzo bowed to no "honkey." Since quitting the guesthouse, he had looked upon the white race with such spite that his insurgent temper knew no control. On nights such as this, he was looking for trouble. And when he saw this man through the flashes of lightning, he only saw the enemy.

The recollection pushed the accelerator lower to the floor, the highway lines shooting by like a quickening heartbeat. Lorenzo had been so high he couldn't see straight enough to aim the gun. He hadn't even felt himself pull the trigger. But the shots sounded off, startling him into taking flight. And when he turned to look back, he saw the man crumpling to his knees.

Broken dashes in the road became a solid flat line. He wondered if he had killed him that night. And if he had, he feared that no matter what he did the rest of his life, his judgment had already been passed. It was a memory so dark not even Nina had known of its existence, carried in Lorenzo's soul alone, to gorge upon his character like a beggar at a banquet.

But the fever dream, Lincoln's words, which told Lorenzo he was alive, and to find him. What did it mean?

"Baby . . . baby . . . slow down."

Lorenzo snapped back. He backed his foot off the pedal, wiped his face with his hand. "Sorry, Nina . . . got lost for a minute there."

Two hands came together over the center console, and stayed interlocked for miles. Lorenzo again looked up into the rearview mirror. But this time, his eyes were caught by the glisten of one broken golden buckle, the top latch on a black vinyl guitar case. Inside was the guitar, the tactile memory. It had been so long since he looked inside the case that Lorenzo could not so much as recall what the instrument looked like. Then again, the owner of this guitar, he could never forget— the one he left kneeling in his own blood.

8

THE SAME IN DIFFERENCE

December

For small-time bands, the Hardliner was long established as a place to go to be found. The recipe that could bring such success was an attitude that shunned the vainglorious tactics of ladies' night, half-priced drinks for anyone in costume. There were no TVs, no pool tables or video games, all seen as disrespectful deterrents from the efforts onstage, as the stage stood focal. The floorboards were worn and gouged. Carnival bulbs lit the edges of the semicircle stage, at least those that still worked. The backdrop was black satin, pocked with cigarette burns from days when smoking inside was customary.

Big acts were reserved for the weekend. The newbie, rank amateur, and yes, a certain Christian rock band, were put up on Tuesday nights, a night habitually relegated to the back burner of the entertainment schedule. But the Hardliner had carved a niche in the community, bringing together on this off night people who shared a predominant purpose, the strong will to be the first to hear something exceptional. Tuesday was a night to hunt for fresh new talent, a band with enough promise to possibly stay etched on their minds when perusing the paper for the flavor of future nightly affairs. And on this night, a night open to all ages, the venue provided three bands, casting the light further underground in hopes of giving rise to those who give it all up in an effort to initiate the spark, fan the flames, and create a legitimate living in the business.

Over decades, the Hardliner never experienced a lapse in popularity, as it was the music that shifted the gears, moved the trends, which brought in the subcultures and countercultures. The motto remained unrestrained and untraditional, from psychedelic rock to indie pop and country punk to thrash metal. Changing genres mixed the crowds, creating a medley within the house that complemented the eclectic mash of bands, seemingly mixed together just to see if it might explode.

Baker, Moby, and Murphy stood at the end of the bar, up against the chrome rail that sequestered four feet of space, the unmolested territory where the waitress could grab her drink orders. Two guys bumped past, bending around the rail in the hope of getting noticed faster. Baker took them for twentysomethings, on the early side, too young and too anxious to get a buzz to know any better. And there they stood, dumfounded that the bartender passed them over time and again.

The waitress returned, holding an empty drink tray in her left hand, her right hand on her hip. "Hey, uh, Ginger."

The guy turned with a grin and went to stroke his strawberry-blond hair on impulse, his yellow Livestrong wristband popping out from under the sleeve of a faux sheep–lined denim jacket. "Hey there, miss, I . . ."

"You see this rail!"

"Uh, yes I do."

"Why are you on *that* side of MY rail!"

The two looked at one another, not paying enough attention to the golden object of such consequence, not moving fast enough out of the way. The guy in the Abercrombie hoodie crossed his arms.

Shouldn't have crossed your arms, signifies disagreement, delay, thought Murphy, looking on.

An East Coast transplant, to be sure, her finely polished fingernails caught the light perfectly, her index finger moving like a maestro's baton as she spoke. "That's called a service bar rail, genius. I'm in the business of service—that makes it MY rail! And if you don't find yourself out of my freaking area, it will be a long sober night for the both of you, am I clear?"

"Okay . . . okay . . . let's not get all hostile over this. Won't happen again, 'kay?"

They backed away, hands up, as she swung into her space.

As she set the tray on the bar, both hands now went for her hips. Her head danced as she continued to scorn the two. "I hope you've learned a valuable lesson here."

He should have kept walking like his pal in the hoodie, but he didn't. "And what might that lesson be, miss?"

Murphy cringed. *Two "miss" remarks, ouch.*

"A lesson on how *not* to be a douchebag." She raised her arm high, palm up. And her bracelets all came jangling down her forearm as she gestured to the front of the bar. "Now go stand out there like those fine people and you *might* get served."

She calmed down by mumbling to herself, cussing under her breath with every other word. Baker caught her eye and raised his glass in respect. She blew a strand of overteased hair out of her face. "Hipsters . . . they just don't know what they don't know, ya know?"

Moby cast his stare out over the crowd. "She's right. Looks like, along with the regulars, we got a lot of avowed intelligentsia from the university here tonight."

Baker nodded to Moby's observation. The gauges, tats, and band T-shirts of the post-hardcore scene clashed with a different look, a contrarily glib style of wealth and thrift.

"That's good," answered Baker.

Moby scoffed, rejecting Baker's opinion out of hand. "Aw, c'mon, Bake. The guys are skinnier than the girls." He pointed fervidly across the floor. "And look, over there, is that a dude or a lady? I mean, these"—Moby made finger quotes—"'revolutionaries' have mainstreamed themselves into an orthodoxy, bruh." After taking a long draw off his one pre-performance house bourbon, Moby wiped his mouth on his sleeve. "And if I see another guy's pinkie come off his bottle of beer . . ."

Baker took a moment to scan the faces in attendance, processing Moby's blunt opinion. A woman wore a trapper hat, paired with a black-and-white checkered scarf in a chic blend of multiculturalism. She hung with two men in beards and Salvy-A flannels, one under a knit beanie, the other a trucker hat, discussing, Baker surmised, the assured existence of Palestine. "That may be true, Mobe, but this tribe pushes societal dogma—they effect change." Baker, knowing all too well of Moby's policy toward strangers, patted his friend on the chest. "So let's not cast too many stones, brother. It's bad karma, ya know?"

Murphy had been taking in the gathering as well, admiring the effort, the crafty experiments of eccentricity. Seeing so many thick black-framed glasses like his own, Murphy wondered how many had twenty-twenty vision. "You know you have something in common with this group."

"Mmmm . . . do tell, Murph," taunted Moby, ready to reject any semblance of simpatico.

Murphy's eyes remained fixed on a guy in a cream Henley and blue suspenders. "Well, Mobe, they are against the grain in every way, at least in spirit. They spend some serious time in self-obsession, on how to be antithetical. For right or wrong, it's why they get out of bed each day." He turned into his conversation. "And what is your style of music, Mobe, Bake? It's a shock to the system. It works for crowds like this.

You just have to convince the alpha opinion, the one who commands a good chunk of the audience."

Moby patted his pocket for a smoke. "I'm not buying it, Murph."

"Well let me ask you this. Does this look like a crowd that will stifle you, your message?"

"God no. Not these newbies. They're all so feeble."

"Look past the physicality, Mobe. It's the mentality, the packaging."

Moby paused, folded his arms. "Packaging . . ."

"Look at the outfits. Every piece pondered upon as an all-important article of personality." Murphy looked to his friends, pushing his glasses up his nose. "And what does Alive and Well offer in terms of presentation?"

Even though Nat wasn't in the conversation, all three knew where he was. They loved to watch him work a room. At the moment, he commanded his own collection of bright-eyed bohemians, who were all too captivated by Nat's character, his nuances, his beaming air of positivity.

"I give you one Nathaniel Thibodaux. Our voice. Our magnet."

Nat held the attention of three women in the immediate, three more on the periphery, who looked to escape their current discourse to see what this captivating man was all about.

"What do you think he's talking about?" posited Baker.

"Shoot," answered Moby, tossing his head back. "It don't matter. These iconoclasts don't generally come across black men, much less a black man of such say-so. This ain't the Big

Apple. Coming across a guy like Natty around here is like coming across a unicorn."

Murphy bit his lower lip, letting it slide out ever so slowly. "He's setting the table . . . at least with the ladies. Not so sure the guys they came with are enthused about the current situation. But it's a good opportunity."

"For what?" asked Moby, now zoned in on his friend, knowing Murphy's brain was firing on something.

"To find the alpha voice."

Baker wasn't one to ask immediate questions, not until he pondered upon the puzzle. He spent a few minutes staring across the room, quietly trying to break some kind of social code. "Murphy, what am I looking for?"

"Body language. In particular, thumbs."

Moby nodded emphatically at Murphy's take, as if marking an appreciation to his jest but knowing his friend wasn't kidding.

Baker, in all seriousness, said, "You mean the thumbs are a tell?" But Murphy went silent in his investigative scrutiny.

Baker scanned over the smorgasbord of wishful artists, musicians, and writers, from those in black everything to the retros who popped in primary colors. He closed his eyes momentarily to eavesdrop into conversations.

The LHC is gonna end mankind.

Have you read Garth Stein?

Spotify? Yeah, sure, I've heard of it.

Obama is sooo cool.

Obama is sooo sexy.

Obama is God.

"Murph, what about over there? Dude in the V-neck."

The guy spoke with his arms folded. His hands went into his armpits, thumbs pointing up.

Murphy held his chin firmly wedged between his fingers. "It's the pose of a superior attitude. But it's too negative to be influential. And he's rocking on the balls of his feet. Either he's lost control of the conversation or his drug of choice is wearing off."

Moby looked down at his thumbs, shaking his head. Societal complexity was not Moby's field of expertise. His snap judgments were quick and final, so he backed away to have a cigarette. "I'm out, fellas. Good luck in finding Mr. Wonderful."

Several minutes passed. Baker looked on, staying quiet, knowing not to interrupt Murphy when he was on a task that posed such a challenge.

Finally, Murphy put his hand on Baker's shoulder. "I got 'im." He pointed from his chest as not to draw attention. "Bald guy in the flat cap."

He was bald but not out of necessity, with only a soul patch of facial hair. His button-down was open, exposing an Elon Musk T-shirt. His hands were slid inside tech chinos, organic cotton, to be sure. But the thumbs were out, pointing not down but diagonally.

"Notice his pose, Baker, powerful and cool. He listens with his head tilted slightly up—he's paying close attention. He leans forward ever so slightly to speak. Unyielding eye contact—that's the guy who stirs the drink around here. That's our alpha."

Baker took notice of his actions, his liquid motion. He was taller than nearly everyone in the room, and he was comfortable with it. His style was simple, as if pulled blindfolded from the closet. And every once in a while, he broke one steadfast rule. In a move that was anything but trendy, he smiled big.

He moved effortlessly into new groups.

"How everyone is so glad to see him," noticed Baker.

"He knows a little bit about a lot of things," Murphy proposed. "He can contribute to many conversations, so he floats among many circles."

"Look how people latch on to him. It's like he has his own personal microculture."

"But there is one person casting a wider net." Murphy gestured in the direction the guy was moving.

He had made his way to Nat, whose crowd grew by the minute. Men and women could make the physical connection with ease. It was the mental connection that was such a gift. Nat's words were joined with demonstrative gestures, lending a certain assurance of who he was and what he was here to do. And Murphy could only cross his arms and take it in. "The spirit of the happy warrior shines bright."

Even as Nat stood quietly, nodding to the conversation, his face rested fixed in an unforced grin. "He is charming, isn't he?" answered Baker, giving Murphy an elbow jab.

Baker sat stage-side in the shadows, to be alone, meditate, quietly pray before his performance. He could only hope his band would be on, playing with a professional purpose that would have their sound roosting high enough above the grade created by the local industry, giving an exemplary outlet to this crowd he hoped was ready and willing to be overwhelmed. He was optimistic that for one hour, Alive and Well would be the ultimate composers, providing the score that would perk the attention of those who listened, allowing all to share in a moment of exultation, where this audience, the bit players, those relegated to the tiny print when the credits roll, can find solace in their own contribution to the success of a small-time band.

When given such an opportunity, Baker knew Alive and Well had to play perfectly. The spiritual message would be shunned, even ridiculed, if not wrapped in the most ear-pleasing sound. Baker and Nat had to walk the line of being piously intense yet fundamentally safe enough to hook into a room of a secular bent, for in a place such as the Hardliner, Christian rock bands had been known to receive taunts under a morass of ill intention. Cars may be left without headlights, tires flattened, if any found their songs to be impossibly triumphant. With only one set to play, Nat would not be granted the opportunity to evangelize during a set break. It was one of Baker's favorite aspects of a gig. But time and place might not present the right equation necessary for a favorable rejoinder. *Next time*, Baker thought. *Let's get our own feet wet before we bring others into the water.*

Alive and Well could not have a more contrary approach than the opening act. Get Lost got by on entertaining antics, playing the role of unruly juveniles, promoting anarchy to the fullest degree with speedy drums and down-picking guitar licks. Each song lasted two minutes at most, but they kept the energy high by running around the stage, through the crowd, creating an air of complete chaos.

The boys on bass and lead guitar played instruments plastered from neck to strap peg in decals, all pertaining to music or drugs in one way or another. Though, what sold them most was their own peculiar appearance. Get Lost began their set wearing leathers from head to toe and black toboggans pulled down to their eyebrows. But as they warmed up, the hats were thrown off, revealing hair cut short and standing on end, each a different color, representing what appeared to be the three flavors of Neapolitan ice cream.

The trio ended to a resounding fusion of whistles and applause, bowing deeply in accordance, just long enough to let such recognition sink in ever so sweetly. As the ovation lost its energy, they hastily pulled their gear to the side, allowing Alive and Well enough space and time to set up.

The first act passed Baker on the stage stairs, fist pumping to the crowd in earnest all the way to the floor. They had set an aggressive tone for the evening, applying all their youthful vigor to run around like unleashed psychotics in a tenacious display of pandemonium. Baker knew his group had a far better sound, but after months of failing to find that perfect marriage with the audience, he had gained a clearer realization that polished play was no longer what it was all about. Within Alive and Well, Nat alone held the embodiment of eye-catching dynamics, and the ability to pull off the ultimate exhibition was now the new glue that stuck in the minds of the younger crowds. It was what they remembered most when waking up with tomorrow's aching heads. Baker swayed to a personal passion during gigs. It's why he performed—for the almost out-of-body experience. But tonight, he thought, maybe a little push-pull interaction with his guitar would personify the sound. Maybe it could pit the raw emotion of the heart against his calculating mind. But as he plugged in, he shook off the thought, as such deliberation would bring him down if stuck too long, for mapping out the experience ruined the natural God-given excitement of never knowing what was going to happen.

To keep with the theme, Alive and Well tweaked the song list, moving the louder cutting songs to the front to piggyback what Get Lost had wrought. As he tuned, Baker knew he would be busy, engaging in a higher dose of string bending and finger picking. And such a forecast had his thoughts splitting time with both excitement and concern, careworn about how much extra tension he could endure, how long before his fingers would break down under such duress and start feeling like they were made of stone, to become stuck in the talon-like pose of a gargoyle until morning.

Alive and Well gave a short warm-up in E minor, a little jam that allowed Baker enough time to loosen the inflexibility that came from inactivity. Upon his nod in readiness, Nat gave a heartfelt thanks to his predecessors before priming the crowd once more, setting the stage for "a different sound, a fresh sound, representing all that is good in the room tonight. We're gonna keep the adrenaline boilin', people, so fill your soul to the brim with love and let's get down to it!"

They fired into "Rhythm King" and didn't stop from there, bridging songs as Get Lost had. Alive and Well, however, created smoother transitions. Moby swept into songs with soft and steady bass passages, teaming with Baker to fade in and out, hoping to put the crowd on a roller coaster that clicked up the slant with slow, meticulous effort only to fall headlong into a pool of instrumental thunder.

They played with intensity but within their own element of taste, keeping things loud, but also smart and honest to their creed. Behind the hard sound, Moby maintained a free-flowing backdrop for Baker's spontaneous improvisations, plucking out his own solos whenever feeling the urge. But whenever Baker and Moby made eye contact, their expressions held an obvious scrutiny of seriousness, a sense that felt onerous, like the effort shouldn't be so demanding.

The looks on their faces were those of discouragement. The music sounded good, not great. It didn't seem to be reaching farther, climaxing the way it needed to in order to break through the barrier to the next level.

Most would have been happy with reaching so high, but Baker had played too long to settle for less. And upon looking up from his guitar, out over the audience, he saw all too clearly the broken connection between band and fan.

Many were moving to the music, but most appeared to be figuratively sitting on their hands in a jovial but perplexed posture. Something was wrong, and Baker knew what that something was.

As he looked back to his drummer, his friend, Baker saw a man far removed from the group, playing with gluttony, just missing his marks. Dolf filled the role of accompaniment, but when asked to drive the music forward, his chops faltered from time to time, not often, but enough to keep the others on edge, waiting for the next trip, unable to concentrate with a free mind to the music and their own instruments.

There was no way to reach him, not on this night. His eyes were wide open, but no one was behind them. He wore a look of calamity as if, when looking out over the crowd, he saw enemies, the pale furtive eyes of wolves. The sticks were pounding away on instinct alone. And without Dolf's brain commanding the drums, his reflex was too regimented to will the changeovers, leaving the others to follow his erratic lead.

Baker felt the heavy heart that came with knowing they had come up just short, again. Alive and Well impressed many. They would have at least a page of newcomers to add to their mailing list. But Baker had hopes of tearing the roof off and shooting the moon. He saw the Hardliner as a springboard to stardom, giving them a strong foothold in the city. What they would get after this performance was only the precarious aspect of short-term success, maybe good enough for the others but not good enough for the man on the Strat, on the tailor-made bass, the aging ones.

Baker's bitterness soon changed to concern for his drummer, a fear that he was slipping too far into his manic episodes, to a point where they would never be able to reel him back in. He had the sinking feeling of coming to a sad reality, a future without one of his closest.

Not wanting to show his disillusionment, Baker put his head down and closed his eyes in an attempt to lose himself in the music, trying to ignore a percussion that continued to come on too strong, Jimmy's synthesizer hum that never quite sat right. The negativity coursed in his veins. He started to feel a quiver in his left hand emanating like white heat from behind the scar.

To get his mind off the torment, Baker did what he always did. He opened his eyes again to watch Nat move about the stage. *How does he do it?* Baker thought. *The one who trudges alongside me through the bullshit every step of the way always comes out so clean and content. I know he can tell things aren't in synch, but he keeps plugging away, tirelessly.*

As if Nat could hear Baker's troubled mind, he looked back to his guitarist with an essence of agreement in his expression, another kind, passive look as if he was telling Baker everything was all right. But Baker could only fabricate a smile back to his lead singer, feeling tragically tired and immune to Nat's normally contagious gaze. *Tomorrow is another day, and I'll meet it the same way,* Baker said to himself, as he had for so many years. Only now, every time he said it, he felt the sting of physical betrayal, no longer able to ignore the possibilities.

With their last bullet, Alive and Well burst into "Be My," playing it how they wanted, for this was their favorite tune and it was Dolf's most polished piece, giving them all a chance to unwind.

> *Won't you let me be your coat rack*
> *So I can hang around.*
> *If you don't get hooked on me,*
> *All you gotta do is take me down.*
> *Why won't you be my top hat?*
> *Let me wear ya everywhere I go.*
> *If you don't like being way up there,*
> *I'll take you down after the show, baby.*

Two onlookers sat along the back wall, paying special attention to the music, feeling the oscillations, the force of faith. Lorenzo rubbed his hands together in satisfied discovery as he broke into his interpretation, breaking down the act to Nina piece by piece in the excitable inflection of a fellow musician on the same pursuit. "These guys are almost tight. I mean, they blow away that first bunch. Too many gimmicks to that first bunch."

Lorenzo pointed to the stage as if he needed to show Nina which direction to look. "See the front three? They show passion. That lead man, he is the straw that stirs the drink. And that guy on lead . . . what a style. He'd lose the pick, use his fingers for speed control. He'd twill his volume and tone knobs and travel the guitar, ya know? Effortless, like the instrument is part'a his body. But that keyboard player there, they probably don't need his sound. But see . . . if you look at his gear compared to the others, all that brand-new KORG and Ensoniq equipment—and notice how small his keyboard is. The smaller the board, the more expensive it is, state'a the art. Ya just know he supplies the PA as well. He's a keeper. For now."

Lorenzo leaned forward, zoning in on the back of the stage. "And that drummer there, he's hittin' his kit way too hard. It's gotta be goin' right through those front dudes, steppin' on their space an'all. Damn near impossible to improvise when you can't hear ya'own monitor. And check it, he's playin' a piccolo snare, an' it ain't tuned for rock—it be tuned for jazz, a brighter sound, ya know?" He paused to notice any other problems. "But other than a few hiccups in the cadence, it's a fine, fine sound. They got promise for sure if they can calm that drummer down a bit."

Nina smiled at Lorenzo's boyish thrill, so comfortably at home within the confines of his own obsession. She took his hand in hers, bringing it up against her heart. "And?"

Lorenzo looked at the members of Alive and Well as they herded their gear off to the side. "They're Christian. Reaching out like strangers in a strange land. Playing with a higher purpose."

Nina pulled Lorenzo closer, feeling the chill each time the door of the bar was opened, far from acclimated to Colorado in December.

Lorenzo gently rubbed Nina's shoulders, grinning wide, large teeth flashing white from his rigid ebony face—his signature expression of affection, a gaze only meant for his love.

Knowing full well quick changeovers kept the crowd gelling, Alive and Well slid their gear off onto the floor to make room for the third band, who went by their guitarist's stage name, Furious Sammy Slide. Baker and the others would stay for the last act unless it was extraordinarily awful, for they had played last enough times to recall all too clearly finishing their set only to hear the equivalent of chirping crickets for applause.

Get Lost weren't going anywhere either. The hyperactivity of the opening act did not fade offstage as the trio, a few years from a legitimate drinking age, sat at the front-most table, igniting their whiskey, dropping it into beer mugs, and guzzling in haste.

For extra effect, the bass player in strawberry hair lit his shot and downed it alone. Some of the liquor missed his mouth and dribbled down his face. He fought back the bile rising in his stomach, completely unwitting of his chin, which flamed like a campfire marshmallow. The lead singer slapped a beer-soaked napkin to the burning skin. "Awww, dude, you're going to feel that tomorrah."

Opting to break the equipment down later, Alive and Well dove into the local masses. Nat sat down in a chair saved for him by Sarah, Margaret, and Genevieve, three friends sipping Diet Coke. The entourage lit up the room with their natural beauty, resulting in unordered alcoholic beverages that had been pushed off to the side. Unbeknownst to the men hovering around them, they were members of Southeast Baptist and were in attendance for one reason: to be fulfilled by the purity of Nat's lyrics, not pickup lines from the inebriated collage of a single mindset.

Nat beamed a wide grin at the features that made his friends so attractive. Beyond their obvious physical traits, their serenity amid such a clamor was a sight to see, for their robust spiritual lives exuded tranquil hearts, setting them apart from most of the crowd through a cultural rift between poise and lopsided obsession. Nat took one of the drinks from the side of the table. He playfully sipped through the skinny cocktail straw, and Sarah gave the mildly scolding look of an overbearing sister who knew better. And she did. *God bless her*, thought Nat. Fortunately, they were bestowed an equal blessing for Nat, a naiveté regarding musical acumen, for the ears of his friends not only lacked the multiple-piercings to adorn more flair but also lacked the ability to decipher the difference between a decent show and a great one. And at this moment, it's what he needed most.

Moby and Dolf went outside for a cigarette. Baker followed but stopped off to bestow upon Get Lost the psychic reward of audience feedback, more curious to see just what they were all about. "Nice job, fellas. That was some heavy, dissenting rock."

Vanilla, the singer and guitarist, seemed unable to contain himself, emitting an inebriated nonsensical response at the top of his lungs, "AAAAGAAHHHH!!!" causing Baker to back up a step.

As Vanilla wished not to lose the complimentary company, his voice quickly descended past equilibrium, inflecting a squeaky pitch that had not yet escaped the grips of puberty. "You too, man. I mean, you play some sweet guitar. And that's a cool Strat you play. You give lessons?"

Baker exhaled out his nose, reflecting on his tutorial days with subtle contempt. "Used to, but nobody ever really wanted to learn. They'd just come in fifteen minutes late like I had nothing better to do and ask to be taught Eddie's 'Eruption.'"

Vanilla grinned in recall of the Van Halen rock standard, shadow playing the riffs in fond memory, to a solo much older than he. "And you could teach it, I'm sure, dude. Your fingering is right on, and that whammy you use is righteous."

Fingering with a little tremolo was always a favorite of the younger throng. Every time Baker used it, heads would rise and start bobbing to the catchy inflection. Baker actually felt it to be a "cheese element" of guitar playing but was gracious in return. "Whatever works."

Strawberry held ice to his chin as he added to the compliment. "I agree, man, you rip. But what's up with your equipment? That amp of yours is so old it looks like it might have mice. How do you get your sound, dude?"

Baker took a brief look to the ceiling before fielding another inquest about his archaic equipment. And it was guitarists who seemed to always bring up the subject, always the ones using the star tools of the trade, the Mesa Boogies, the Marshalls. Ironically, on the local scene, the best musicians owned the most inferior gear.

And Strawberry, the proud possessor of a powerful Hartke Kickback, was right. Baker's Peavey Classic 50 was on the brink of classification as an antique. With little more than volume and tone knobs, its appearance gave an obvious impression of ultimate deficiency. This dinosaur was topped off with an equally ancient Traynor pre-amp. There may be only ten people in the world who could generate a full sound from this combo. Baker was one. It all fulfilled his technological compulsion to tinker. He folded his arms. "If you guys have a few hours, I'll tell you how I pull everything I can out of those cabinets."

The three looked blank, suggesting disinterest. Baker took the opportunity to catch up to his boys, unable to squelch a peculiar fondness for the members of Get Lost. He would pray for them.

As he slowly pushed through the crowd, he received his usual attaboys from the true music fans, more buoyant and demonstrative from the Christian-music following who frequented their shows. While he gave thanks to all who graced him with encouragement, his hand went to rub his neck, signaling—in a mannerism Murphy had come to know—that tonight, Baker felt the praise was undeserved.

He passed the small out-of-the-way table the Hardliner put out for anyone wanting to leave their name and contact information. Leaning over the table, scribbling his details, was the tall man in a flat cap, the alpha. His shirt sleeve was drawn up just enough to show a tattoo on his wrist, and Baker knew immediately what it was, a Chi-Rho, the sign of Jesus Christ, the same moniker Baker wore on his outer forearm. As if feeling Baker's presence, he looked up, meeting Baker's stare. And he grinned, giving a nod as if he could read Baker's mind.

Alone with Dolf, Moby had the opportunity to talk of his performance. But he felt mentally tired, not into a hostile confrontation, for showdowns with his drummer these days were becoming bold acts of bravery, with iffy results at best. He chose to leave the assessing and counseling to Baker, who had an uncanny knack for speaking softly and teaching volumes.

Baker, Cecil, Murphy, and Jimmy joined the two outside. The band as a whole maintained a legitimate level of sobriety during the more important gigs. Jimmy, however, was sped up, as usual, with his teeth grind in full swing—the telltale sign of cocaine bumps in a bathroom stall. With Jimmy the Mole, it was a question of merely functioning in a public place. He was so full of anxiety and doubt that Baker could not yet reach him entirely, only able to slow down his cravings through motivational speeches or, more likely, a sterner warning of physical damage from Moby, who had his own problems with alcohol.

But Jimmy's vice flew under the radar, a classified annoyance compared to Dolf, who was far more difficult to keep straight these days. He had been drifting with more regularity, becoming distant like a stand-in who really no longer knew his mates that well. His depression was accelerating, as everyone feared, quickly turning into a noticeable progression, leaving behind the once-hopeful hypothesis of being only a phase.

A keen eye had to be kept on him at all times. At no moment was he to be left alone. Separate from the others, Dolf slipped into episodes of hostility and reckless behavior. If anyone happened to look at him with any semblance of a challenge, there would almost surely be ramifications. Alive and Well was exiled from Tippler's due to a brawl solely induced by the troubled drummer. They were to never again darken the door of Lusty Monk's either, the sentence for breaking the nose of a fraternity boy who nagged Dolf for spending too long at the urinal. Two key venues scrapped, written off at a tremendous loss. Baker couldn't help but begin to wonder if Dolf's face was behind a thumbtack on the office wall of every booking manager in the city.

But despite Dolf's short fuse and the growing separation between him and the band, his work ethic was unrivaled. He never missed a practice, never neglecting an opportunity to slam down on the heads of his drums with pronounced purpose and precious release. He never wanted a session to end, and Baker, at first, thought it admirable that Dolf had such drive. But his adamant orders to stay and play soon became disturbing, a matter of galling annoyance. Once Baker and Murphy saw the mad-dog anxiety in his eyes when he put the sticks away, they began to put the pieces together, now realizing he was afraid to go home, to be confined to his inner world where the voices could be heard, the growing hallucinations seen with such clarity.

This fear forced him to spend the night at Jimmy's with regularity, beating on his drums alone long into the darkness. Even for Jimmy, who embraced late night like no other, it raked on his patience. With the racket going on downstairs, he couldn't hear his television set.

And at the Hardliner, the insatiable need had manifested itself once again, as Dolf kept angling for one more song, one more song. Baker and the others obliged with reluctance until Sammy Slide finally approached the stage, giving a sign to quit by drawing a finger across the width of his neck in a slow, deliberate manner. When Baker turned to Dolf to sew up the last song, he could see his drummer staring Sammy down through his cymbals. He could feel the chill running down his spine, thinking with trepidation that his friend was most likely envisioning beating the guy to within an inch of his life.

The scene hung heavily on Baker, and Cecil noticed that he was sneaking peeks at Dolf the whole night, as if trying to look into his brain, seeking answers. Over the years, Cecil had become part of the band as if he stood on that stage himself. The challenges Baker and the others faced were the most exciting aspect of life, and he would forever saddle that merry-go-round of uncertainty, serving as fuel to the engine that kept them chugging along for just one more show—for it was the best ride in town, bobbing hands-free on the good nights or holding on tight as it twirled out of control during the bad, feeling that if his grip ever gave in to the force of strife, the whole circus might come to an end. And no matter who came out for the circus, it was always a steady good time.

A quiet remained over the group as they traded glances with one another until breaking up in laughter over their plight. How ridiculously difficult it all had become.

Murphy was the first to show some optimism. "Grow through adversity, gentlemen."

Jimmy took the opportunity to recycle an equivalent remark from the video library of his mind. "Endeavor to persevere."

Moby gave Jimmy a solid punch to the shoulder. "Hold up, I know that one, Mole. Uhh, Clint Eastwood, a western, uhhh . . ."

Jimmy cowered. "C'mon, Moby, that hurt, you asshole."

Baker got between the two before Jimmy could make the mistake of retaliating, draping his arms over each of them, and the rest joined in to close the circle. Baker dropped his head and the others followed.

On that stage, you hear our voice.
On that stage, we lay our requests before you
and wait expectantly . . . Amen.

They all stepped back into the Hardliner for the last act, except Dolf. He remained pressed against the bricks of the club, gazing down lamp-lit Broadway, a look of worry across his face. He was afraid to go back inside. He was afraid to stay where he was. And he was terrified of going home. Another long, arduous night lay ahead. He looked for a liquor store, for the liquid vitamin that could help him find balance until he could pass out cold.

Lorenzo drove his Mustang north along Interstate 25. The vehicle was a real eye-turner in its beach-cruising heyday. But the first winter in Colorado had taken its toll. The front right fender showed the marks of his first wreck, when he had slid sideways, ramming into a concrete barrier. It was pressed so far inward that Lorenzo had to use a crowbar to pull it away from the wheel so it could rotate freely enough to get him home. Though, the front wheels shimmied a great deal anyway, ever since Nina had hit her own patch of ice, which sent the car over a curb. Both accidents had been discounted for lack of experience, as neither had ever seen snow before.

He tapped his fingers along the steering wheel to the likes of Max Roach, bringing himself down from the impressions of the night, the sensation that the band Alive and Well had given him.

His own musical sense allowed Lorenzo to see past the minor flaws in timing and tone, feigning any great regard toward the overall lack of stage presence. And in seeing the possibilities buried beneath the mistakes, Lorenzo couldn't get the look of dejection on the guitarist's face out of his mind, unable to help but feel sorry for him. "His dream has become a crusade."

"What, baby?" said Nina, half asleep in the passenger seat.

"The guitar player in that band, Alive and Well. See, I can tell the lifestyle is chislin' away at 'im. It's just sad's'all. Maybe he should give in a little. Maybe the ideal is too much to overcome."

"And you think he should give in?"

"I don't know, Nina. When you have such a talent . . . I mean . . . he's got a better chance of success than most."

Nina rested her head back on the window, tired from a long day of work, a night of play. Lorenzo took hold of her hand, caressing it up against his smooth face, in loving appreciation that his Nina stuck it out with him so late. "But they are brave. They have a purpose." Max Roach brushed on his drums, and Lorenzo hearkened back to the steel of his first instrument. "Without direction, the devil will get to you through your vices—and aimlessness is a vice."

"Yeah, baby, it sure is," Nina murmured sleepily as she felt the sweet comfort of the new life they were building together surround her. "It sure was."

9

IN FROM THE COLD

Ever since the day Nina walked through the door, T & R's Salon began to pull them in again, albeit slowly at first. But soon word of mouth flowed throughout Five Points about the new girl in town, the heaven-sent talent who could fulfill your every wish. Within only weeks, the three stylists amassed a clientele they could hardly handle, a following Thelma and Regina had only fantasized about, for not only were their salon chairs now regularly occupied, but "sistas" populated the waiting area as well, coolin' it with juicy gossip and fashion tips until it was their turn, once again feeling close to one another amid their sanctuary off Welton Avenue.

Nina was working on Monique, a new customer of late, who had arrived crying a day after seeing a freelancer.

Not feeling that she had the money to afford a real salon, Monique had gone to her neighbor. She was able to provide a relaxing atmosphere, and the greens and beans she served up had been delicious, but from there, it all went downhill. Her friend's good intentions were commendable, but she just couldn't deliver, leaving braids that were far too tight, giving her the worst headache on earth.

Nina was mortified, feeling grief-stricken for Monique's situation. "Girl, you must be going through hell in these locks. Here, take some aspirin."

Monique threw back three pills with a glass of water while Nina gently massaged her stinging scalp.

"Sista, we need to get you out of those 'fore your roots are gone."

Nina proceeded to meticulously unfurl the twists. When her hands began to cramp, Thelma jumped in for a time. What had taken six hours in the kitchen of a kindly amateur would take two days to undo. But when it was all over, Monique would come back to T & R's from then on.

Nina fixed every screwed-up job in town, from base knots that could be seen a block away to twists that came undone to flop in the wind, or any other contrived fix-me-up that might lie hidden and fuzzy under the most-chic hat. Though, beyond the problem hairdos, Nina had her regulars. The corporate women came in for a conservative flat twist, bringing their children in shortly after seeing such a kickin' style. Athletes at the nearby high schools came in to get plaited up for basketball season. And those without yet a care in the world would arrive to be wrapped and threaded, as Nina took care to give each head a unique character, that individual statement, which embraced the careless attitude of youth.

Thelma and Regina lost a few customers to Nina, but it was all for the good of the salon. The two learned more from their new employ than they could ever have taught their young prodigy, not believing such old dogs as they could ever learn any fresh sleight of hand. It had taken Regina a while to warm up to the fact of being a bit outdone, a little put off by Nina's quick rise in the profession. But stubborn pride eventually waned at the sight of what Nina had done to her own hair, giving Regina long cornrows, braiding the ends to—as Nina put it—dangle free and dazzle.

Nina had a surprising business sense about her as well, a clever intellect that moved the salon further along a path toward success. She put forth an idea of adding a few partitions. "I don't think women are too hip to being on display when they've lost control of their 'fro."

She proposed dropping the price on more extravagant styles. "We've got our niche down to a science here. Not to overstep my bounds, but I think we can make a statement as well as a nice profit. Five Points ain't exactly Fifth Avenue, know what I mean?"

Nina accumulated menus of the local restaurants, those that would deliver to the women who waited. She also became friendly with a caterer. "I don't know 'bout you girls, but I get awful hungry during some'a these marathon sessions."

And Rumeal's African shrine on wheels rolled by during the busiest hours, always leaving a stocked display in his wake.

The tortoiseshell hairpins were a hit, as well as his extensive selection of kente hats.

Before long, the salon became *THE* hangout. Women from the community would just drop in to chat, bringing the latest dirt to dump on anyone interested. Downtown kitchens were suddenly vacated, forcing any man of the house to "fend fo' his own self." Suddenly, there was more to do than toil away over a hot stove. After all, Oprah was always on TV at the salon, and it was much more fun to watch as a crowd.

To any potential customer peeking in, it may have looked like a logjam in the waiting area, but to see the "superbad" styles walking out the door would make them want to do anything to get inside, to join the club, for the benefits of this open-to-the-public sorority included superlative exclamation on a woman's own individual look, bestowed by the girl with the God-given talent. Everyone wanted to know where this heaven-sent gift to the coiffure came from. It gave Thelma and Regina the opportunity to brag about how they rescued Nina from the throes of poverty, all the while realizing it was Nina who had saved them not so long ago.

During a midweek snowstorm, within the empty confines of their dream business, two aging black women had been flipping through *Ebony* and *Jet*, chattering back and forth about what had recently been sent down the grapevine, rehashing memories of the fried "wigs" they had as kids.

But what was really on their minds, what was ceaselessly grating at them, was the one question that had gone unanswered, the question that was so tired as not to be uttered any longer, only kept deep inside like a festering wound. *Whatever happened to the salon we saw so clearly as a nirvana for the black women of the neighborhood? We did everything right. What did we do to deserve such a fate?*

Thelma and Regina were steadfastly attuned to the traditions of their culture. They followed their philosophy of the perfect Afrocentric salon to the letter. They kindly catered to any who rang, but even with regulars spanning decades, with daughters of the original clientele and lineage extending three generations, the bills were outpacing revenue.

There was a time when income was brisk—when T & R's had stylists. Thelma and Regina, with four busy employees, gained the confidence to sign a five-year lease. This way, rents could be locked in. It made good business sense. But there would be competition that was unanticipated, not something a small-business owner could buffer against. Such an expectation wasn't a trend found in trade magazines. Unbeknownst to them, Thelma and Regina were training their future competition. And the best were staking claim all over Five Points, each taking a chunk of clientele with them every time the door swung closed for the last time.

For those who were offered a chair inside the doors of T & R's Salon, a spirit of family was offered upon the staff. Thelma and Regina would reach out as matriarchs for many of the women under their employment, many of whom grew up struggling in single-parent households. Through a long-standing relationship within the neighborhood, they were able to hold out against the new salons. But to their dismay, a challenge came from an even greater threat. The impressionable young women of the salon would fall victim to the word on the street, the smorgasbord of welfare programs that awaited all who applied.

"They make more sleeping in and watching daytime television than earning an honest livin' stylin' hair," Thelma would pose.

"Scoffin' at an honest day's pay, for shame," answered Regina.

"Dignity stolen like a thief in the night."

The best friends bounced their dejection back and forth, day after day.

"How do we compete against the deep pockets of guv'ment, Thelma?"

"Bigots, Reggie. S'all they are. Bigots with low expectations based on the color of our skin."

That's usually where the conversation ended, with no idea how to get out of the hole bored out not by these women but by suits in front of microphones, feigning emotion on television to cobble together a few more votes.

Soon their staff returned to two old women, watching as the last under their employment left to be raised by the powers that be. "It's just another plantation! Trust in God to supply your needs," Thelma would plead, watching another woman of promise succumb to living for the check at the end of the month, listening to the sweet nothings from the bureaucratic purveyors of "social justice."

The loss of each stylist hurt more each time, as it represented one less prospect to possibly take over the business. Thelma and Regina were too old now to take on the task of the sixty-hour workweek. Their physical limitations would eventually lead to a substandard effort, a disappointed client. But it would not take so long as to lose clients through a bad result. It simply took the women too long to finish the job. Customers were in a hurry more than ever. They would begrudgingly find an alternative, picking brevity over meticulous effort from those who cared too deeply about the trade.

Storefront windows were cracked. Cold air eked under the entry as weather stripping dragged the ground like a hound's tail whenever the door opened and closed. They couldn't bring themselves to complain about the deferred maintenance. Rent was being paid in a combination of dollars, home-cooked soul food, and a growing stack of IOUs. Their landlord was a kind man, but the favors he granted raked on their last nerve. They were proud women of business and would find a way to make things right, somehow.

Regina, a type 2 diabetic, could not be on her feet very long. With the growing pain, Thelma had taken over most of the mundane aspects of salon work. She set her Windex bottle on the counter next to the feather duster and joined her friend in the empty waiting area. Regina was lost in concentration, staring down the street as she watched a young black girl stop for a brief moment outside the doors of the clinic. Regina sat forward, one hand over her mouth, the other plucking at her knee-high panty hose.

"Oh, Lawd. Don't do it, child," she whispered to herself. "Look to your heart, move on. Dear Jesus."

After several minutes of contemplation, the girl went inside, and Thelma took Regina's hand. "Another baby will return to God. Let's pray for that girl, Reggie."

This had become almost a daily ritual, ever since Planned Parenthood took the corner of their block. Regina felt as if she could see the baby's soul floating up to heaven, and her heart broke to pieces each time as the two women leaned into one another and called upon the Lord to forgive.

Thelma let silence fall around them. She had to let the moment settle in before she could bring her friend back. After several minutes, she rose up to get a snack, for noshing on Thelma's baked goods always lifted Regina's spirits. In little time, Thelma recaptured her attention. They were amid a rant about their childhood, about their mother's old style of crowns built by underbraids, sporting bangs in the forties fashion, when the buzzer rang.

Regina slowly slid out of her chair. Muffin crumbs caught by the ledge of her large bosom fell to the floor. She shuffled over to answer through the microphone, a security system procured to keep the riffraff, the crackheads, out. "Can I help you?"

A young woman, looking somewhat out of place, stood on the other side of the smoked glass. "Yes, well, ma'am, I'm lookin' for the owner of this here salon."

Regina looked back to Thelma. "Ma'am? Shoo. Is this girl lost?"

She smiled back to the visitor. "That would be me, hun."

"I just moved to the area, and, well . . ." She cocked her head in hesitation. "I'm lookin' for a job, as a stylist."

Regina laughed in acrimony through the mic. "Girl, you see any customers in here? We barely got enough patrons to pay the bills, much less eat. I sorry."

Thelma scampered to the door as fast as the old woman could, cupping her gold-ringed fingers to Regina's ear. "Girlfriend, look at her locks, they gorgeous. And she don't even have a proper coat on. She's shakin', for Lord's sake. Let her in already."

Pouting at her friend's request, Regina hit the entry button. The door murmured the cue to pull it open. "Come on in, baby," Regina said with indifference, the way she spoke to travelers seeking directions and cops who shoved mug shots in her face.

"Thank you," said the young lady, relieved for any brief ease from the weather.

"Have a seat here, child," said Thelma. "You want some hot tea, somethin' to eat?"

"No, thank you, ma'am," she answered, despite the pangs in her stomach, which had shrunk for lack of a proper meal.

"Now you can just cease with that ma'am talk, honey. This here's Reggie, and I'm Thelma, okay?"

"Okay. And my name is Nina, Nina Dehere."

Thelma burst into a belly laugh, showing off the roomy gap in her front teeth. "De-hair. Ain't that the truth."

She couldn't take her eyes off Nina's beautiful black locks, coming forward to gather a little of it in her hands, letting the braids fall between her fingers. "Did'jou do this yo'self, Nina?"

"Uh-huh." She paused. "But I can do all kinds of styles, weaves, micros, interlocks. Then there's what I think you call goddess braids, Casamas braids?"

Thelma stepped back in surprise. "You can do those?"

"Sure."

"Shi. Reggie here can't even do goddess braids. She gets evry-thang so tangled up it comes out lookin' like a—"

"Oh, you hush up now," spouted Regina.

Thelma went to the counter to fix Nina a cup of chamomile tea despite her initial refusal. "You're so young, child. Where did you learn to braid like that?"

"My motha, my sista, other women of my village."

"Your village?"

"Well, we called it a village." She did not want to delve further. "It was just a part of Florida, a part you've never heard of."

The two women sat back down, crossing their arms in silence. As they peered at Nina, trying to figure out her story, crow's feet gathered in the corners of their eyes, revealing the true proximity of their age. Nina sat cradling her tea. Unfazed by their staring, she patiently perused the salon. The roots music and the lush plant life relaxed her. She had noticed Thelma's and Regina's hair to be natural, nicely done.

The old women were struck by a certain power in Nina's face, so seriously taut for a woman so young. She sat erect, with confidence, unlike someone who looked to be battling every day to stay afloat. Nina had been through a lot in her short life. It was an intuition learned by Thelma and Regina over time. They had heard every hard-luck story of Five Points over the years, ranging from episodes not reaching beyond small talk to the more substantial dialogue, as the women embraced the pressing need to be the therapy to anyone's burden.

"Where do you stay, Nina?" asked Thelma.

"Sometimes the Y. Sometimes we find an all-night prayer room. Sometimes our car."

"Our? You have a man?"

"Of course she has a man, Reggie! Look at her."

Nina smiled. "Yes. His name's Lorenzo. We came out here together. He works the loading docks on Denargo Market. And he plays in a band."

But Thelma wasn't listening, too lost in an impassioned gaze, mesmerized by Nina's onyx-sharp eyes wrapped in copper, seeing in them much of her own self as a youth. Suddenly, her motherly perceptions took over, despite never having children—two abortions as a teenager had left her infertile for the rest of her life. "We might have a place for you, hun. We have a back room that—"

"Thelma!"

"It's all right, Reggie. She could sweep up. And it'be good to have a man around at night to look after the place."

Regina put her hand to her chin, thinking. "I guess she *could* sit in the waiting area. With locks like those . . . could bring in customers."

"And she could teach you how to set goddess braids," chided Thelma.

"Girl, you better stop with all that, 'fore I come over there and mess you up."

"What'choo perpetratin', sista? You just better stay sittin' put and take yo' medicine."

Regina got up surprisingly quickly, approaching Thelma with arms raised. They started into smacking one another playfully.

Nina had laughed at their antics, liking them from the start.

In the hours between ten and six, the time when the three were together, they became close. With just a trickle of heads to style on a daily basis, Thelma and Regina got to know Nina well, or as well as she would let them.

They met Lorenzo, saddened to see sharp cheekbones protruding through his kind smile and a scrawny frame that struggled with carrying paltry duffel bags from the car. Though, dampening these physical shortcomings was his genuine courtesy and overall gratitude for the accommodation. Through stoic eyes and a general vein of gravity in Lorenzo's posture, Thelma and Regina soon realized they were in the presence of two lovers bent on survival. For now, Lorenzo was reserved to nibble on morsels provided by his musical ambition, until things started tilting in his favor. And such an attribute was welcome to stay at T & R's Salon, for ambition always leaked that vibe, reminding the two elders of their own dreams.

Nina continually reminded her new friends that they would only stay a little while, until they got on their feet. But it didn't matter to her employer and landlord. She breathed a certain fire into the two, a feeling they had been missing, forgotten in a life that they grew to know as customary, with only one another to hold on to. So Thelma always responded to each promise the same way. "Don't you fret, baby. You're welcome to stay here as long as it takes."

The buzzer echoed through the salon, startling Regina, for it didn't buzz often enough.

"It's Ruby!" she said, almost dropping her plant mister.

Thelma put her hand on Nina's shoulder. "Now, Nina, this is one'a our best customers. She comes in every coupl'a months to get a trim and a shampoo."

Before buzzing Ruby in, Thelma turned to her partner. "Now mind your p's and q's, Reggie."

"Oh, hush up."

The plump regular entered with a slow shuffle. Thelma took her coat from her shoulders. "Ruby. How are you today, girlfriend?"

"Oh, baby, the nap patrol has been beatin' on my psyche. I tried sleepin' in sponge rollers, but I ain't got the expertise or the patience, know what I'm sayin'?"

"Well that's why we're here, honey. Now you go on over to Reggie and she'll fix you right up."

Ruby waddled over for a consult, slipping in between the arms of the chair, just barely. As Regina dove into her feel-good spiel, Ruby spied Nina in the mirror. "Well who do we have here?"

Nina raised her hand from the broom. "My name is Nina, Ruby. Nice to meet you."

"Girl, those are some beautiful extensions you've got there."

"Those aren't extensions, Ruby," interrupted Thelma. "It's natural. She did it herself."

"Get out!"

"Fo' real."

"Come here, child. Let me get a closer look."

Nina walked over to let yet another impressed woman pick up and examine her hair.

"Ooooo. I wish I could have hair like dis."

"You could," said Nina.

Regina's eyes bugged, aghast at the statement. She had been unable to do more than color and texture Ruby's hair since she first arrived on their doorstep five years ago. "Uh. What she means, Ruby, is that you know we'll give you the finest cut in town, guaranteed."

But Ruby remained fixed on Nina. "Can you give me a new look, Nina? I mean, I don't have da hair I used to, but could you do something with dis bird nest? Dis dry and tangled mess?"

Nina looked to Regina, Thelma. They stood frozen in horror at the possibility of losing a regular.

"Come here, baby. Tell me what you think."

Nina grabbed a brush to see what kind of length she had to work with. Pulling through the snags, she got Ruby's hair to drop to her shoulders. "Let's see here."

Ruby noticed the look of concentration in Nina's eyes, making her feel like the most important woman in town.

"I think some flat twists would make you look divine, Ruby. I would have to use some lin extensions at first, but if you let it grow, we can take them out in no time. Let me show you what I mean."

Nina took a fashion magazine from the table and flipped through a few pages. "Here you go, Ruby. Whatta ya think'a this?"

Looking at the style Nina had turned to, Ruby glowed in utter excitement. She probed on at the pictures with her chubby index finger. "Oooo. Oooo. That one. Or no. That one there. Can you do that?"

Nina stepped back with hands on hips. "Girl, I'll have you turnin' heads all over town. Yo' nevva gonna hear so many compliments."

Ruby belted out in a brassy Baptist choir voice. "Hallelujah! Girlfriend, my wig is at your service."

Two hours later, Ruby couldn't stop looking at her reflection. "Can I see that hand mirror? I want to see the back again."

Her flabby arms swayed to and fro as she rotated the mirror around her head. "Nina, child, you surely are heaven sent. Wait 'til the girls see me at church. They'll just flip, I tell ya, flip all over the place."

Nina looked at Thelma, who couldn't wipe the grin from her face. She pointed a playful finger at her first customer. "Now, Ruby, like I told you, this'll last about two weeks. I want to see you back in this chair then, to keep you stylin' and profilin', ya hear?"

"Baby, you'aw the fountain of youth. I'm gonna tell all my girlfriends about you."

Ruby popped out of the chair, sporting a new walk to go with her newfound beauty. Thelma had her coat. "Now you listen to Nina, Ruby. Do what she says and the nap patrol will be a funny memory, ya hear?"

"You got it, sistas." She gave Reggie and Thelma high fives as she strutted out into the day, a new day, as if she was living a dream.

Lorenzo found weekend work playing in a jazz band. They were a collection of old-timers. They played the small cocktail bars and eateries or under any roof open to the improv these senior citizens felt compelled to act upon at any given moment. It was nothing funky, no fusion, only cool jazz, an Art Pepper or Chet Baker kind of vibe, the kind they had grown up with, forming their own dissonant styles as kids born out of the discrepant times of the Civil Rights movement.

For lack of room to store a drum set, Lorenzo had put off looking for one. The room at the back of the salon was bigger than what they were used to, but only in that it was about the size of an eight-man tent, a safe haven for personal possessions, but no more. Once he and Nina found a permanent residence, Lorenzo would then look for the perfect instrument. In the meantime, he only unloaded an extra set from the trunk of Earl's, the saxophone player's, Lincoln Continental. It had belonged to Zak, the former drummer who died recently, of pneumonia and other compounding afflictions of old age.

It was a dated acrylic model from the midseventies, cosmetically maintained with carefully applied nail polish and auto finish. The set was older than its new drummer, but it had its advantages, for the biggest benefit to playing such a dinosaur was the ease in preparation. Only having one sweet spot made the toms and snare a breeze to tune. As for the bass, a few shredded newspapers were all it needed before Lorenzo was ready to play. After each gig, he would load it back in the same trunk only to be reunited again at the next club.

Even with the different style, so much more complex than reggae, Lorenzo gained a knack for jazz quickly. The new form left much more room for experimentation, pushing him to play more off the top of his head, maintaining a poignant yet effortless tempo.

He wasn't asked to do anything extra for the band, merely to perform on calling, like a freelance situation. But come time to play, he became the young leader. The crowd's attention would be on the overall sound, but the band was with Lorenzo as he soon learned to direct improvisations with nothing more than subtle changes and eye contact. The old men loved the freedom the boy provided, as he kept things interesting, accenting any instrument that may be tugging on him that particular night. It soon became obvious the others would never have to worry about their new drummer; he was solid, just like their old buddy Zak, only decades younger, and getting better night after night.

Lorenzo's day job consisted of loading and unloading produce trucks. It was physical work, toil his gaunt, out-of-shape muscles could barely tolerate, leaving him lifeless at the end of the day, less creative when having to play drums at night. He tried to find other work, but he lacked experience outside the labor pool, where the uneducated mixed with the illegals, ex-cons, alcoholics, and junkies, a class he'd driven halfway across the country to escape.

Another new laborer was hired on a month after Lorenzo's first day on the job. A month meant certain tenure in this field of work, and the young new blood named Tommy Lingo knew right off who had been around the longest. He sat by Lorenzo during lunch, trying to get the skinny on the job, wanting to know the shortcuts, where and when he could half-ass his way through the day.

Before the noon break, Lorenzo had watched Tommy for hours, finding it not too difficult to sum up his imperfections. He was a weak white kid with a body of baby fat, a shaggy redhead who carried a speech impediment, using words no one had ever heard before. For lack of learning and general cultivation, his mind was smothered in ignorance, wrapped tight in a plastic sheath of moral dilemmas. Lorenzo thought

Tommy was most likely his mirror image of a poor background, for it was obvious he had experienced more tragedies than triumphs. His mind was full of misguided schemes, dreading and hating all rules or constructs, which created fuzzy boundaries around decisions that might make him more civilized.

He pulled out a jelly sandwich and a Pepsi. Between bites, Tommy took sadistic pleasure in hurling stones at alley cats that had their butts sticking up too far out of garbage cans. Lorenzo only listened to piecemeal bits of Tommy's one-way conversation, growing tired of attracting every wayward misguided soul to his stoop, the place where he tried to eat alone, in peace. He wanted to get up and rid himself of the unwanted company, but Tommy had come looking for company in his weird awkward way. So Lorenzo reached back to get his newfound Christian wits, the patience of a saint. That's when Tommy got into a slurring digression on his last job at a pawn shop off Speer Boulevard, working under a man named Parrish, "the jerkiest nutwad th'ever was."

Lingo explained his duties as to have been a genuine slice of hell. But it didn't sound like a bad gig to Lorenzo, probably regular hours under a roof, out of the cold. *The pay couldn't be much worse. How bad could this guy be anyway?* he thought. *It's not too far outta my way to see if this so-called nutwad Parrish might have a sign in his window, lookin' for somebody who could work circles 'round Tommy Lingo.*

Lorenzo drove straight over from work the day after seeing the *Help Wanted* sign posted in the window, barely discernible through the muddy slush thrown upon it by rush-hour traffic. As he opened the door, clamorous bells overhead shook his body, intensifying a headache that had been growing all day. He pointed a finger to the window. "I seen this sign and wondered if I might be able to work here."

Parrish, the venerable proprietor and boss, looked up from his newspaper. He carefully folded it together and set it down. A farting sound came from the plastic cushion of his stool as he rose off of it, pulling down on his blue polyester slacks, which had ridden up on his crotch from hours spent in a sedentary posture. With a huffy look on his face, as if he was put out by the disturbance, he slowly stepped out from behind the counter. Lorenzo tried to reach into himself for a little vitality, just to leave a good impression, but he couldn't help the way his arms hung, his slouchy posture, beaten down by a day of loading fruit baskets for the Christmas season. The hard labor had left everything out in the open for the owner to size him up, and in this owner's mind, the kid didn't amount to much.

Parrish stood eyeballing Lorenzo, breathing with a wheeze out his nose. Lorenzo could see that he had been a big man at one time, though now his broad-shouldered frame only held remnants of what he used to be. His clothes wreaked of tobacco, and his chimney-red nose always flared like he smelled them. He was careless for sure, since a butt of a cheap cigar dangled from the corner of his mouth. His hair was the color of a gloomy winter sky, like the city sludge amassed curbside. Even his face was ashen, but these displeasing features were subordinate to his captivating powder-blue eyes, like perfect robin eggs dotted black in the center. Lorenzo chose to look upon them in a hope that maybe they exposed some form of undeniable kindness beneath his veil of sick displeasure.

A younger Parrish might have seen this as a responsibility put upon him, to shape this youngster into someone to be proud of, but not anymore. He simply looked him up and down and ran through his now-so-habitual procedure, laying out his "take it or leave it" policy, listening to nothing the boy had to say.

Lorenzo surely didn't blow him away during this informal job interview, for he had never had one. He only tried his best to keep his head high, eyes forward. When Parrish was finished fleshing out what the job entailed, he stood still in another moment of disquieting silence. His face read plainly that he looked upon Lorenzo as no better than the usual short-timer, a typical kid between jobs, who would only show up until something better came down the pike. Parrish had seen it all too often. Anymore, no one dared tempt a fate of having to own up to a career as a pawnbroker, for a stigma had latched on to it over the years. The business now stood next to loan sharks and bail bondsmen in the imposing light of mistrust and overall filth. It stood next to cracked and rusty barber poles as a depiction of a bad haircut from some ancient coot who couldn't stop shaking enough to cut a straight line.

But being an astute student of an old-fashioned way, he decided to bring the beaten kid on for no other reason than a look Lorenzo had, a gleam that still showed fire behind flagging eyes—that and the reality his back wouldn't last another day of moving inventory alone. *Anyway*, he thought, *he has to be better than that slacker I canned the other day.*

As Parrish waited for Lorenzo's answer, the decision swam around in his mind, willing to wager with anyone on whether this kid would even come back, all the while trying to figure out when the day was that work ethic lost its meaning.

After the Second World War, Parrish, then a green but optimistic war vet, had pooled his funds and bought a defunct laundromat off Speer Boulevard. He kept the overhead low by living in the loft above his new business, and with such a prime location, Parrish's Pawn was soon brought to fruition, becoming as active as any five-and-dime around.

Locals came to know him, came in to chat—chat about how friggin' cold it was or when it would ever stop snowing. Conversations with a poignant tone became the order of the day, and Parrish forever lent an ear. As he saw it, "Anyone could render a bit of fact or warped philosophy on anyone, at any time, so listen up."

It was fair to say Parrish was an extraordinary card player, and it wasn't long before he cleaned up the back room of his shop, making space enough for a few extra tables and chairs, designating the dimly lit chamber a nightly poker club. And as word got around, it began to pack in ringers and ploppers every night, becoming so popular that a late arrival could only droop across the makeshift bar and wait for a seat to open, drinking cheap whiskey as his payday bankroll grew heavy in his hands.

Suddenly Parrish was keeping constant company. The back of his store became the life support of every transplanted Hebe, Czech, Pole, Ruskie, Negro, and Chicano from Colfax to Santa Fe Avenue, like an auxiliary VFW for his brothers-in-arms. Some brought their wives, but most came to conceal their whereabouts from them, for the back room of Parrish's Pawn was a virile refuge. It was where the boys played fair, where winning or losing came in a distant second to hearing the latest on Fairweather Al's bout with the Smiths' Doberman midway through his morning postal route. Or Buddy the Breather's latest stop on his Peeping Tom tour, where the lady liked the rough stuff. The stories flowed like sand through war-torn fingers as they recycled themselves on an endless conveyor belt, coming back slightly distorted from the guy who told it last. And upon weighing out all the truths and exaggerations, the most outrageous tales were sure to be challenged by a few dollars laid on the table, from someone needing legitimate proof to bolster even the slightest belief.

But as years passed, time began to change the flow of these simple people. Pressures replaced the devil-may-care attitude. The future pushed toward center stage. And with every revolution of the year, fewer friends came to occupy the Salvation Army chattel that surrounded the green-felted tablecloths. Four games became two; two became one. One became a lackluster excuse for a good time. The hard-core who remained just had nowhere else to go. They were all alone now, staying only for the roof over their heads as they wagered pennies and talked ugly tales of the hereafter.

Regardless, Parrish was steadfast in providing all he could to his companions. He gave with all his heart, and they took it with innocent greed, oblivious to what they had grabbed hold of, pulling Parrish down with them in that back room, now a vacancy, housing only empty souls.

So many friends lost, lost to the creeping tick of the clock. Terrance went peacefully, dreaming of an ace up with two in the hole. Georgie fought back three heart attacks before a stroke dropped half his face, leaving him with a misshapen appearance wished on no one. Ivan lost his mortality to a drunk driver as he walked home with a nice jingle in his pocket. And Manny took a plunge right into Parrish's ever-popular homemade burgoo. The place broke up in laughter, thinking it was the Polish rum. But things got quiet when no bubbles came through the broth.

The realization of the compounding grief he would endure by the deaths of his comrades never occurred to Parrish, not in the beginning. They were his family. But every passing took a little more out of him. He began to pray not to be the last one to go, but his words fell on deaf ears. The finish line appeared too far off on the horizon, like a mirage. And how could he ever get there when he was eternally burdened with bearing someone else's pine box, a regular pallbearer wishing he was the one inside, resting horizontally, forever.

Lorenzo accepted Parrish's half-hearted proposal, extending his hand out to his new boss. But Parrish only turned away and headed for the counter, to sit behind the same register he had opened over fifty years ago, mumbling to his new hire to go home and rest up for a busy day tomorrow.

There was no need to inform his old boss that he was quitting. Laborers predictably came and went at the docks, readily replaced by the next in line. And just knowing he didn't have to return to Denargo Market gave his mind and body an instant feeling of relief. Lorenzo broke a few traffic laws driving back to his room behind the salon, anxious to tell Nina of his new job, and those fascinating eyes stuck in the face of such a "grumpy-actin' old man."

10

BROKEN BRAIN

February

Bartending by day was an easy choice for someone with the temperament of Nat Thibodaux. But it was only a means to keep his loftier aspirations in the air. His true north was to live with godly intentions, and he was determined to have these aims bound to a life in music, dreaming of a blessing for his discipleship by way of a career that would one day support a wife and a big family.

With a father serving his country and a mother tending to the needs of his four brothers and sisters, personal responsibility came early for Nat. It had to. And his parents prepared him for the challenge, giving him a firm roof over his head, where he realized the unconditional love of family and the Heavenly Father. The Thibodaux's went to church service twice a week, ate at the table together, and spun records by

Mahalia Jackson and the Soul Stirrers as Nat harmonized in perfect pitch with his mother, often bookended by his father's warming baritone and the thin falsetto vocals of his little sister.

It was all the sustenance he needed to succeed on his terms. Now in his mid-twenties, he was armed with common sense and the courage to fail. And fail he had. But as spoken by his father from half a world away, as a man who had seen his share of horror, "Experiences aren't good or bad, son. Experiences just are."

The funds compulsory for a college education would have stressed the family budget, leaving too little for his younger siblings. But this would not deter a man with a drive to learn and the creativity to make it happen. There may not be a diploma at the end of Nat's master plan, but he would be the first Thibodaux to attend college, even if in such a non-conventional way.

Nat moved to University Park, shared an apartment with University of Denver undergrads, and attended the classes that interested him. He carefully researched his professors, finding those who practiced in the profession they taught so as to lecture on firsthand experience. These were the people Nat sought, not the tenured sort who floated along in the academic pools of self-aggrandizement, seen by Nat as nothing more than ego trippers in water wings, eaten by sharks if ever venturing beyond where they could not touch.

Over the course of two years, he lived life as a student. He joined student groups, attended parties, and stayed quiet and attentive in the back of class. He gained a greater understanding of music theory, psychology, philosophy, and theology. He learned French, and took astronomy just for kicks. He spent late nights in libraries that had it all.

Nat had asked his mother if he was stealing his education. She never turned from the dishes she was washing. "Will this help you to shape yourself into a person who makes this world a better place?"

"Well, I think so."

Nat's mother turned to her eldest child. "I know so, baby. I know so." She then commenced to flick soap suds at him. "But you give back when you're able, Nathaniel. Balance the scales, ya hear?"

Nat went aside his mother, to grab a towel for drying. "Yes, Mom. I will."

Nat could balance a checkbook and change his oil. Capitol Hill Baptist hosted free EMS classes, and he took them. He used personal experience and a free education to obtain a diverse and thoughtful way of contributing to a conversation. He would say what he meant and spoke with meaning, for it did not require a certain age but a level of maturity, understanding gained by living hand to mouth, living life to its fullest by way of a survival instinct ingrained in everyone, but used by few.

He wouldn't bartend just anywhere. It needed to be a place that would feed his desire to absorb the beneficial attributes of others. So he occupied the space behind the bar of Achilles, where the producers, the tech developers, and the

CEOs convened. The result became a drawer full of business cards of the most premium stock.

Indeed, a good starting pay with benefits was guaranteed to a man with a public high school education and a spotty resume. Nat had no diploma, no GPA, no accolades from a higher education to flaunt in a job interview. But when he described his college experience and the way he went about it, eyes lit up on the other side of the bar. Jaws went slack, for such an idea had never crossed their minds.

"You're a survivor, Nat. Come see me when you're ready," said the head of an indie startup.

"What a ballsy thing to do. We'd love to have you on our team," added a sales exec.

Nat had countless contacts on two-by-fours that would be a college grad's dream. But who was it that held all the cards and could lay them down like so many royal flushes? A kid who would be perceived by many to have had limits. But these perceived confines were merely monetary, material means. Nat knew the true validity behind his own pursuit of happiness, which needed nothing more than the wits ingrained in him by his mother and father and a spiritual road map drawn through a daily covenant with the Almighty.

Behind the bar of Achilles, he was surrounded by talent. He would listen and learn, taking the opportunity to add his own two cents when it came. To be sure, Nat was one in love with his position in the universe, feeling confident in his ability to make each customer feel welcome and at home. He was mindful of what his regulars liked to drink and what they liked to talk about. He could be the comic or the straight man, the spokesman or the ear. But on rare occasions, someone would fall in off the street, someone who didn't fit the mold of the normal clientele. On this day, such a man was Dolf.

"Ay, Nat," he barked, "if you don't cut down on the foam, I'm gonna jump back there and start pouring my own."

He didn't speak in such a manner when he first arrived. Promptly at 11:00 a.m., Dolf had bounced through the door. With arms outstretched, he approached the bar and leaned over to give Nat a hug. And he was happy to see his big pal. But once Dolf slapped a healthy stack of bills on the bar, Nat knew he would be sticking around a good long while.

Dolf worked when he wanted. He was the best at what he did and was paid in kind, for skinning logs was back-breaking toil—not only was the job not for everyone, but it was for hardly anyone.

Timberhaus Inc. offered a spot to any warm body willing to put forth the effort. But they kept the want ad running, knowing the type they drew would rarely make it to a full paycheck. Most who took on the task were the college tough guys, aspiring to reach the level of "mountain man." After all, they bench pressed 325 and squatted two "cookies" more. But pushing iron in the temperature-controlled environment of Spandex pants and wall-to-wall reflections could not pre-pare them for the ultimate in manual labor. They seldom endured more than three afternoons, as the constant pull of the draw blade, using muscles they never knew they had, grew redundant and tiresome. Only the Hispanics stayed for any length of time. And by association, Dolf had learned just enough Española to be dangerous.

Employees were compensated by length. The faster one could remove the bark from the twenty-foot timber, the greater the compensation. Some of the most ambitious greenhorns might inquire about overtime. And Jake, the super of the crew, would just break up in hysterics, asking if they had brought their own supply of Toradol before sending them out to Dolf, who would show them how to utilize a chainsaw without losing a digit.

Since Dolf first stepped into Jake's trailer, after passing an interview that called for little more than a pulse, he was the only hire who had remained in a trade where the revolving door twirled nonstop, each laborer departing by way of a sore back or worse. For Dolf, however, it was the perfect job. He was alone with the raw material, to tear into it with reckless abandon. Those who could afford to own the cabin of their dreams wouldn't stand for industrialized speed. No machines could give a log the look of the frontier, a look that came from a man who toiled mercilessly, giving it that much-desired Jeremiah Johnson appeal. And so, the majority of what came off the line of Timberhaus was at the hand of a burly, seasoned one-man gang, with headphones pulled down snugly over his ears, speaking only to a brisk wind, a stingy knot that protruded from an otherwise finely cut surface.

Dolf had made his money earlier in the week, breaking his old five-day skinning record by ten feet. He would have continued on but was undressing logs faster than the trucks could bring them. Jake had enough raw material to last through the next month and had to plead with his modern-day John Henry to take the day off.

Before the bar filled with the afternoon crowd, Nat had some time to spend with Dolf. They weighed in about music, Marvel versus DC, the first impressions they had of each other.

"Well," started Nat, "your size was quite evident, and those meat hooks at the ends of your arms, all scraped and cut up. I thought you might have tossed a caber or two in your day. Maybe boxed kangaroos, wrestled alligators or somethin.'"

His fingers could barely slide through the mug handle as Dolf lifted the glass toward his anxious lips and then wiped away the sudsy mustache on his shirtsleeve before starting in on his recollection of meeting Nat for the first time. "You weren't preoccupied with yourself."

Nat pulled back and smirked. "Whattaya mean?"

Dolf brought himself to make brief eye contact. "You're put together, Nat. You take care of yourself." He took a long, slow drink. "And you're so self-assured. It's guys like you I think about punching, hard, you know, in the pretty face." Another drink. "But Baker introduced you to me, and I trust Bake. So I knew you were the real deal."

Nat pondered the thought of being on the receiving end of Dolf's right hand. He balled his own fist and sarcastically punched Dolf in the shoulder. "Must say, I'm glad it went the other way."

Dolf had only a subtle reaction to Nat's playful gesture, a facial cue by way of the slightest smirk that conveyed an understanding, before a faraway gaze took him to a deeper place. "Over the past few years, I've watched you. I feel the energy come off you, always optimistic, always encouraging. No complaints, expecting nothing. Just living a life with grace." Another long draw. "I try to find even a morsel of what you have. Some way to ease up on the throttle, coast, if only for a few minutes." Dolf paused. "A few minutes . . . that would be nice."

Before Dolf's thoughts could lapse further into the abstract, Nat gripped his friend gently on the forearm. "The arch of the moral universe is long, Dolf. And only the righteous can stay upright against all the problems, all the strife. The only way for it to bend back in our favor is through humility and love." Nat squeezed as if to bring Dolf to attention. "Understand this, my friend. The highest view of God is the solution to all that troubles you. Don't try to take on your difficulties alone." Nat looked to the other end of the bar, where customers were gathering. "Hey. Sit tight. I have to attend to my other guests." But Dolf had gone dark, his face paled in his thoughts.

Over the next hour, Nat tried to further engage with Dolf, but he seemed to be out of body, staring through him, as if existing in a parallel universe, at least until his glass was empty. Only then would Dolf snap back long enough to order another, thrumming his fingers, setting and resetting his tattered ball cap until another glass arrived, to return to the yoke that embraced his soul.

Unable to convince Dolf to leave, Nat kept him on beer, trying to buy time while waiting for help. But Baker was working on a deadline, a renovation job in Boulder.

"Hang in there, Nat. I'll be there as soon as I can," he'd said.

Dolf had become intoxicated with a look of mild insanity. Such a pose had cleared the rail of anyone who had come in for a late-afternoon relaxer. Nat's regulars had retired to tables as well, far away from the instability, from danger.

His posture slumped, but his eyes were now raised to the surroundings. He glanced up at the wall clock over the bar, squinting at the hour hand, willing it to move fast enough to get to the evening's gig across the street.

And move it did, from the one to the three, but Dolf didn't notice. He hadn't taken his eyes off the yellowed antique face to see any action, too fixed on watching nothing, waiting for something to happen. The tick of the clock was inaudible over the house music, but it sounded nonetheless, a strict deliberate pulse in his head, so out of sync with his racing mind, feeding his manic episode.

Dolf mumbled incongruent thoughts aloud. His head dropped to focus on Nat, who could sense the warm gaze on the back of his neck. He felt his skin tighten under Dolf's unblinking eye. But Nat could not help but feel a deep sense of sadness welling up inside, for his friend carried pain that was not of his design. His conduct was not that of a conscious effort. And for this, Nat felt a deep regret that he had run out of ideas, ways to bring him out. He only returned to his concentrated effort of dunking and redunking clean glasses into soapy water, wiping down a bar that already shined like a new copper penny in the first place, praying for a divinely inspired way out of the situation.

Baker looked after Dolf when he could. And when Dolf had called at an odd hour of the morning to see if he could hang out, Baker's gut churned over what the prospects of day-off idleness could mean. Then Nat called with a plea for help. And later, Dolf called with another invitation to join him. Now later in the day, Baker picked up on the stammering pace of Dolf's voice. Knowing he might lose whatever faculties he had left at any minute, he dropped everything to drive back to Denver.

This wouldn't be the first drinking establishment where Baker would need to pull Dolf out. And he knew where to look each time—the bar, end seat. This is where he found him, easily ascertaining Dolf's state by what sat beside his elbow. His chessboard was laid out and set up, and men had been moved in a logical strategy, but no one else was playing.

Baker gave Dolf a firm slap on the back, bringing him out of his trance. Dolf sluggishly raised his head, giving his eyes a moment to focus. "Eyyyy, Bake, how ya doin'?" he slurred.

He pushed out a stool for Baker to join, and he sat down carefully, with the wary understanding that he might have to diffuse a bomb. "What are you up to, Dolf?"

Pushing away from the rail, Dolf looked at Baker with close-set eyes, slightly crossed. "Well, as you can plainly see, I'm as busy as a one-legged man in an ass-kickin' contest."

"No," rebuked Baker, not getting the answer he wanted. "What I mean is, what are you doing? We've got a gig tonight."

Dolf smiled under his veil of drunkenness and responded like a true do-gooder. "And I'm early." He drummed his fingers on the rail. "Ready to go."

Before Baker knew what he was doing, he gripped Dolf's arm, digging his fingers into his tricep. "This isn't the way it's done, man. This isn't some kind of game." He picked up Dolf's beer mug. "It's not *this* kind of band." He drew Dolf closer. "Listen to me. When I invited you on this journey, I saw talent, and someone who might gain the capacity to take up the cross and all the suffering it entails. In *you*, I saw the required strength."

Baker thought of Dolf's mental state. Should he bring it up, or would the outright madness be used as a crutch to bludgeon his point? He chose the disarming path of questions over statements. "Are you worthy of your suffering, Dolf? Do you still have the guts to rise above your outward fate? Because fate is chosen, my friend. Is yours going to conquer you, or are you going to achieve something transcendent through it? Can you become courageous? Can you become dignified in the face of your own destruction?"

Baker didn't know he would blurt it out, but his and the band's concerns of suicide had been attempting to break out into the open for months. He paused to see a reaction on Dolf's face. But on this occasion, he felt he was too late, failing to get through the maze of disjointed thoughts from a man preoccupied with fear.

In a fit of frustration, Baker grabbed a corner of Dolf's chessboard and pulled it out from under the pieces, but unlike a magic act, the men flew everywhere. Patrons close enough to notice were struck by such a daring display, though no one moved, including Nat, who froze at what he had not anticipated. He now saw two outcomes, one ending with Baker flying headfirst across his bar, the other with Dolf getting it, and making for the door.

"Get up, Dolf."

"Wha?"

"I said get up!"

Nat watched as Baker crossed a line and into a situation they had all avoided with dread and despair. But in Baker's mind, it was warranted. He was willing to take it for the group in an attempt to get through to his falling brother.

And to Baker's dismay, Dolf rose to meet his demands, looking down at him with crinkled brow. "Now, buddy, you're not thinkin'a starting a conflict right here, right now, here in this fine establishment, are ya?"

Baker neither blinked nor fidgeted under the ominous descending attitude of a man seemingly twice his size. He simply went up on his toes and pointed a wary finger. "You take it for what you like. But if you order one more beer, I'm going to have to do something about it."

Nat studied the subtle reaction in Dolf's face. And to his surprise, his muscles went slack. Baker had presented the resistance of some immovable point, a situation brought on by the worry and love of a friend. And the freight train of animosity simply slammed on the brakes.

In an instant, Dolf's light died within him; his faculties dwindled by the mass of the moment. The confrontation brought all his wretched agony out in the open. He had lost his strength, releasing the reins on his emotion. He always kept the worn-out catchall excuse of blaming it on the booze in his back pocket when he got hold again. But through the fog of insobriety, he saw he was now faced with a profound destiny.

Baker cringed in sympathy as Dolf blurted out sentences that untied themselves from any meaning. His anger was overcome by sadness as he watched Dolf's vain attempts to get ahold of himself. Half of him wanted to break Baker into pieces, and half of him wanted to cry on his shoulder, and with such polar perplexities from which to choose, he crumbled into his seat, no longer able to cope with the challenge. Dolf soon settled into a passive state, getting hold of his disorder like one gets used to the dark, growing more comfortable by not seeing clearly but seeing enough just the same.

Dolf was deep in the throes of tragedy, in a sickened state—a situation Baker knew needed professional help. But it was help that required Dolf to have enough concern to seek it out. His remaining friends provided all the support they could, but they were only the equivalent of fleas on the back of the rabid hound that was Dolf's tortured mind. On his own, Dolf could only hang on until the rage slept, until he could catch up to his runaway mania and manage a grasp once again. But when the beast awakened, it would turn on him again with seething intention, leaving Dolf to drop all restraint and run for his life. The aggravation attributed to playing such a diabolical game led to an intensifying hatred for the world, which ran an extensive course right through almost anyone. But there remained a few he could not harm, yet. And his fury wavered before one of them.

"All right, Bake, I give." Dolf grabbed his ball cap from the bar in a clenched fist and made for the exit. But as he passed his adversary, whom even in his present state Dolf recognized as an ally, Baker noticed tears welling up in his eyes. And Dolf proceeded on with a parting Baker was surprised to hear, in a clarity that nullified doubt. "He's the Grandmaster. I know it's over in seven moves. He knows it's over in seven moves. I can only prolong the game with the moves I have left, moves being forced by the one winning the game."

The statement told Baker that Dolf was well aware of what was happening to him, and what little he was able to do about it.

"Dolf, why don't you come back to my place? I'll make some coffee. We can just talk."

But Dolf only held up his hands, a look of shame crossing his face. The last of his faculties were tied to a feeling of humiliation. And a stubborn pride pushed him away, to the door and out into the street.

Baker let out a deep sigh, trying to step out of the situation and release the pressure on the adrenaline he had just binged upon while standing six inches under Dolf's nose. He bent over to pick up the mess scattered over the floor.

Nat's palms pressed his temples, finding his relaxed center again. "Well that was fearless."

Baker hobbled around in a stoop, swelling the leather sack with each playing piece he pressed back into it. Nat rounded the bar to help.

"I think to be fearless might be irrational. Just played the odds, s'all," Baker said.

"And what odds did you give yourself?" Nat inquired, reaching under a table for a black rook.

Baker rolled up the chessboard with care, making sure it wasn't too tight but tight enough, just the way Dolf would have put it away. He then looked around one more time at his feet, making sure he had found every one, all of Dolf's little pals. "Fifty-fifty at best."

Baker scratched at his beard that had grown out over the course of the winter, keeping an eye on the door for Dolf's return. After a few minutes, he gave up, turning his wonder and worry to what might become of the evening, what he could have done differently. Baker looked back to Nat, who was finally shelving all the glasses he'd been washing over and over. "No one in here would believe it, but there is more to the story than what they've seen today," he said.

Baker gathered up what was left of the money Dolf had left on the bar. Folding the bills, Baker jammed them in his front pocket. "Even the helpless victim of a hopeless situation, facing a fate he cannot change, may rise above himself."

"I'll pray it to be true, Bake. It'll be okay. We'll be okay."

But the corner of Baker's mouth turned down. The two most optimistic members of Alive and Well held the five aloft, but the weight was now so substantial as to make their knees buckle. And Baker posed a question, asking more with desperate eyes than words.

"How about you, Nat, are you okay? I mean seriously, how's your heart?"

Nat rounded the bar, put his hands firmly on Baker's shoulders. "Do not be anxious about tomorrow, for tomorrow will be anxious for itself. Sufficient for the day is its own trouble." Then Nat backed up a step, waiting until Baker's eyes met his. "I'm good, Bake," he said with a smile. "I'm good."

That night, upstairs, Jimmy was busy trying to make sense of the galaxy of cables that lay in haphazard coils across the stage floor. He had to keep his mind off the fact that they were still missing a drummer as he tore into the equipment trunks in search of the "damn electrical tape!"

Nat and Baker sat at a table offstage, staying well out of Jimmy's way.

Nat took a sip of warm tea. "So if he gets here, what kinda drummer are we gonna get?"

Baker looked at Jimmy the Mole as he dug through the gear, leaving it spilled out all over the place like so much overturned dirt. "Who knows. He's in a severe state of mind right now. A way we'd never seen before. But he needs his instrument. It's his way to get out of his head for a few hours. I really don't think he'll pass on the opportunity. Unless he's unconscious somewhere."

Nat used Baker's shoulder as a crutch as he got up to go help Jimmy find what he was looking for. But before releasing his grip, he turned back to bow his head. "Oh, angels of God, enlighten our friend on this night, save him from evil, and set him on the path to salvation."

"Amen."

Downstairs, Moby was beside himself with anger. Sure, he drank with the best of them, but never before a big gig. He sat close to the entrance with Murphy, fidgeting in his chair, watching the door for his drummer.

"How's everybody doing up there?" inquired Murphy.

Moby stole a swig of Murphy's Dr. Pepper. "Man, if anything ever ran normal, I swear I'd drop dead."

"I think it's a test, Mobe. The strife is multiplying the closer you get to the calling Baker has brought upon you. And it will get worse, if you let it." He took his drink back from Moby. "I like to think a breakthrough is coming, Mobe. But before you advance, your mettle will be tested." Murphy's glass created a small pool of water on the table. He took two fingers and pushed through the pool. He made circles that created the effect of ripples over the surface. "You need to remain obedient, and patient. You can only find solace by the grace of God. Once you find grace, the door will open for you."

"I'm gettin' tired though, bruh. This five-piece band seems to be a few too many souls to get pedaling in unison. I'm a jerk for sayin' this, but sometimes I think of just quittin' altogether, *finis*, ya know? Maybe try to live a life of predictable stability."

Murphy consented to the feeling but said nothing in agreement. He'd been along for the ride as well, not quite ready to start all over. "That's Latin," Murphy said.

"What?"

"*Finis* is Latin. It has two meanings. It means either 'the end' or 'a goal to reach.' If you cancel your goal, can you define your existence?"

"I know my goal, Murph. It's where Baker is. That's where I want to be. His faith is strong. His will is second to no one. I have my vices, my rude nature. Excuses and blame still roll around in my head. Then I see Baker hide his pain, and I see such conviction. He doesn't lash out against the friction. He doesn't condemn God for his suffering. Why is the path of someone living so righteously so difficult?"

Murphy put his elbows on the table and leaned into the conversation. "Moby, Baker found God *through* his suffering. And in it, he finds the most direct communication with Him. He is able to die for Christ every day. And in doing so, he can live fully."

Moby leaned back, as if the statements pushed him against his chair.

Murphy continued. "You're basing Baker's life on human experience, human tradition, and human merit. Living in Christ has no place in this analysis. *We* are the temple of Christ. And Baker has been able to put the Lord's House first."

Again, Moby stopped to think. "You know. What you just said. You said 'has been,' not 'is.'"

Murphy was now moved to ponder Moby's statement, caught in his own unease. "He *is* only human. His spiritual healing has beaten back his physical, his earthly challenges. For God, the power to heal is constant—the variable is faith. And a variable by definition is erratic . . . as life is erratic."

Moby let his face drop. "Everything hangs on Baker's ability to push forward, dragging some of our crass identities along with him. I feel like the resistance is too strong. Like we're sliding backward, about to crash, and no one can reach the emergency brake. No one."

Baker saw Moby and Murphy in a deep discussion he did not want to interrupt. He needed to step outside to turn his brain around, away from the brutal intuitions that swam rapid laps, punching the wall, bouncing back and forth over a pool half full, half empty.

Small snowflakes danced in the streetlights, swirling in the blustery Denver night. Baker felt as if caught in the globe, shaken by large hands. He grabbed for the support of the ice-cold railing of the fire escape, squinting past the nature of the situation. Through the winter display, he noticed a dark figure stepping with purpose toward the bar. He watched his stride, trying to notice an intoxicated wobble. To his relief, Dolf was negotiating the distance between them with little trouble.

But his eyes looked dark and distraught. The face affixed to Dolf's body was that of a stranger, a sullen unemotional expression of suffering.

His complexion was like a marathoner deep into the race, pale and sick from exertion, yet running with a desperate purpose, with no time to catch his breath, for Dolf had also come to know that if he were ever to stop, he would let the destructive illness catch up. To rest was to let the voice yell in his ear with a free-lashing tongue, gnashing teeth speaking mental violence in a guttural tone, stirring him awake to begin another mile.

Nothing needed to be said, or Baker didn't know where to begin. He could only put his arm around his troubled friend and lead him inside.

Moby had enough chastising verbiage for Dolf to fill a novel to the density of *Crime and Punishment*. But seeing the way he looked under the blanket of Baker's affection, Moby wiped the pages clean. He tried to crack a smile, but his expression came across as if he had just bitten into an onion. "Good to see ya, bruh."

In what resembled a funeral parade, the two at the table followed Dolf and Baker up the stairs and into a night of restless doubt.

Nat, with his inbred knack for good cheer, could come up with nothing other than to offer his hand. But when he took hold, Dolf's squeeze was cold and limp, falling out of Nat's power grip like he was made of water.

Jimmy walked up briskly to see what the huddle was all about and, lacking the tact for the situation before him, ranted, "Well look who decided to show up. Where the hell have you been, man? You about drove me half-crazy tonight, you know that!"

Dolf only looked over Jimmy's head, toward the stage, giving a weak grin at his remarks.

Put off by his drummer's ignorance to his question, Jimmy jumped up and down, waving his hands in front of Dolf's faraway stare. "Dolf, are you in there? If you can hear me, CAROL ANNE, RUN TO THE LIGHT!"

Dolf noticed his gear had already been brought up from the truck and knew without a doubt which of his friends had taken the trouble. "Thanks for bringing in my stuff, Jimmy."

But Jimmy only snorted at Dolf's appreciation, walking away in a huff. "No problem, dammit."

Without further delay, Dolf was on top of his dismantled set, working with purposeful haste. His concentration reappeared like someone had snapped their fingers, bringing him out of his absent trance. "I'll be ready in ten minutes, fellas."

Baker and the others looked at one another, befuddled. Not sure what to make of another sudden mood swing.

Club Nomad had an in-house soundman. Murphy didn't mind. After a long day in the cold, he was content to spend the evening throwing in as part of the crowd, joining B.A., who beamed in anticipation. Murphy craned his neck, looking about the room, happy to see such a big gathering. Not knowing much about the venue, he was puzzled at the surroundings, the variance of age and attire. The walls were covered in black 3D wave acoustic wall panels. Black leather couches lined the room, with high-top brass tables to the rear, secluded booths in the corners. Beer was served in bottles, with a chilled glass on request. The well-dressed men drank Manhattans; the women drank nothing Murphy could recognize, only that many came with flowers, edible flowers.

Then there was the dichotomy of who Murphy would consider the all-nighters, guys and girls who came early, stayed late. These patrons would throw peanuts on the floor, but the floor was polished, wide-plank Brazilian redwood, Murphy surmised, unapparent that such bar fare had ever hit the surface. They gathered together. They all knew each other. They strode the area like they owned the place, and the kempt patrons tried not to stare, eyes flashing at the perceived gatecrashers as not to be caught. Murphy was at a loss.

"This was the old Brix and Styx," said B.A. "Was the oldest pool hall in the city." Pressing a newly chilled glass to his cheek, he grinned at the sensation and took a savory swig. "This place was the preeminent juke joint. Ole Mr. Joseph Cobble let me stock the machine, new selections every month. The old man let his customers pick the genres. He would walk over the list the first of every month like clockwork. That's how the beautiful old guy functioned, like clockwork."

"So, what happened?"

"Age took hold. Left the place to his kids, and they flipped it overnight to a California investor. The investor turned it into something for the West Coast migrants, and the rest is history." He pointed around the edges of the room. "And all these guys and gals are none too happy about it."

"Looks like a healthy component of the West Coast Techsodus up front," Murph surmised.

"Yeah. The younger throng of the old school consider them a menace. But heck, these newbies from the 650 left for the same reason I did, to escape a dumpster fire." B.A. looked to the ceiling, through the ceiling, to his Creator in a personal habit of repentance. "But I was once a 'lefty' too. I thought I knew everything when I was my *own* god." Leaning back, B.A. put his hands upon his substantial belly. "It's the ultimate hypocrisy, really, fanciful self-pleased do-gooders flicking ideologically lit matches on the dry tinder of hard-earned tradition . . . and never looking back at the consequence."

"So what you're saying is, this could get interesting."

"At any time," answered B.A. Leaning back, he interlocked his fingers behind his head. "Yup . . . at . . . any . . . time."

Murphy turned his attention to Dolf, so zoned in on his gear, tightening and loosening the tension rods, leaning in with his ear, tapping the heads.

Murphy flipped through pages of diagnoses in his head, thinking of a bipolar disorder, schizophrenia at worst. *The only way to block out the state of delirium is with physical aggression*, he thought. *The skinning of logs, hitting his drums, it anesthetizes him from his recklessness.* Then his thoughts turned to the Catch-22. *There's no way the guys have a chance to make it with such a time bomb. They're going to have to let him go sooner or later*, feared Murphy. *Then how easy is it going to be to look after him?*

Murphy noticed Dolf's eyes, bugging with intensity, ever so bent on beginning the night, causing his heart to grow heavy.

Though B.A. wore the guise of a simpleton, Murphy's mannerisms were not lost on him. He took Murphy's hand, and they bowed their heads.

"Almighty God, they stand humble before you. They seek you out to take away all that troubles. Take them away from the difficulties knocking on their mortal souls. Be their hedge of protection, and release them of their frustration. Show them the way. Amen."

And each rose up slowly, Murphy, B.A., and Cecil, who sat so stoic as to be unnoticed, but in participation just the same. Planting his knuckles on the table, Cecil mouthed an additional silent petition to his Father in heaven before catching up to his friends.

The stage was as stylish as the room's surroundings. Pin lights cast beaming spokes down along the scalloped swags of the backdrop curtains the color of deoxygenated blood. Gold ropes pulled the sides back, tassels hanging as boundary lines to stage left and right. Cutting-edge LED lights with moving heads were affixed to the rim of the stage. A single step down allowed the vocalist easy access to the floor, to explore the crowd as Nat was inclined to do.

On this night, he chose to don a black skullcap over the shadow of hair that now grew from his scalp, donning his sharpest leather vest with no shirt underneath. Putting the prospect of a sporadic beat behind him, Nat greeted the crowd with a spirited salutation, pointing at those sitting closest to the stage. "Mmmm. Mmm. You people are looking fine tonight. Lemme just say, it's a pleasure to be playin' here at Club Nomad." In good faith, Nat always tried to prop up the headliner but couldn't for the life of him remember their name. Some Cabaret something or other.

Looking over the room, Nat was pleased Alive and Well had a good turnout from their staunchest fans. A lover of Christian rock simply wouldn't find many extreme faith productions about town. Club Nomad wouldn't pull much of a bar tab from them, but Alive and Well would thrive on their spirit, with minds melded to the intention.

Then there were the former fixtures of Brix and Styx. In memory to Old Man Cobble, they had made "Uncle Joe" huggers with the owner's likeness on the side. When another round of beer arrived, they raised a hand to the waiter, rejecting the enhancement of the frosty glass. Rather, each pressed the bottle inside their foam memorial, raising their brew in honor of the long-time proprietor. "Salt of the earth," they would say, a guy who would allow them to sleep one off in his back office, who cared enough to drive someone home when driving was impossible.

Indeed, they were present to raise a little hell in an attempt to take back a nightspot once theirs. But most on this night owned the contrary aura of the establishment, West Coast transplants faithfully in wait for the second act.

Upon sizing up the variant crowd, the band agreed to start slowly as not to startle the apathetic state of the nouveau riche as they waited for what they'd come to see. But as Nat continued with his introduction, the closest tables jabbered with one another, over his words, and such curt behavior raked on his pride.

Such carelessness toward his greeting impelled Nat to alter the game plan. With a quick look back to Dolf, who was positively attentive to his lead singer, Nat held up four fingers, indicating a jump to a later song. And with the expressive nods of agreement from the others, he turned back to those indifferent with a last word. "I'd just like to ask a favor of y'all out there. If you can open your hearts . . . and open your minds . . . we will not let you down with our sound. Sooooo HIT IT!"

Dolf was right on time with the crack of his snare, and instead of coming in one after another, Jimmy, Moby, and Baker dove in together, creating a volume that rippled the surface of every settled cocktail.

> *This slippery session is all so fast.*
> *This interpretation leaves me so lost.*
> *To be is hard enough in life's fat lesson.*
> *Got no pen or paper, just a lot of questions.*

Chatter continued to pour out of the dapper mass of socialites, warring with the music in muddy speech under the dominating resonance, forced to either conquer by yelling, give in to the music, or leave.

Those who chose the contemptuous route had to lean in close to hear the gist of conversation. Others closest to the stage rose up to escape what they considered racket. Yet some remained, if only to save the prime seats for the next band, though they questioned their decision as soon as a horde of experimental youth in nose rings, hip chains, and Caterpillar boots plopped into the abandoned tables to have a bit of fun with their new neighbors. They rubbed dirty elbows against linen sleeves, winking in playful attraction at their dates. They screamed and stomped heavy feet to the beat and the good fortune of the front row while the well-groomed group in witness to such fanfare only sat now so quietly, necks sinking into pressed collars, brioche scarves. As the rough crowd danced, bouncing off tables, they gripped their wallets and purses, sipped their drinks more often in an unsettled, orally fixated chagrin, unaccustomed to such a free-falling descent from high class.

Nat noticed the enjoyment many were having, happy and carefree. He motioned to double up on melodies that were working, leaning into the mass of bodies, singing directly to a cute brunette, hair streaked with purple, who flashed a big smile at such attention. Meanwhile, Baker played the chords, always slightly different, channeling his emotions rather than what had become rote. Improvising his play, his mind was free, allowing his performance to be ad-libbed by the hand of the Holy Spirit. And as the floor fused with the wild bunch from a bygone venue and the Christian stalwarts, Baker felt lighter upon a buoyant rush of optimism, that this show might become the next small victory, the next brick in the road.

Dolf had been consistent all night. Only minor chinks in the meter had occurred but were expected whether he had been drinking or not. But Moby was on top of it, alert to catch any problem, covering any glitches by laying down a dependable groove until his drummer could get it back together.

As they performed "Would You," obliging Dolf by playing longer once again, the headlining act exacted themselves in front of Alive and Well as if to say, "Cut the crap, get off the stage, stop thieving our spotlight." This band was used to being the focus, their fans were waiting, and they didn't like what they perceived as being shown up by an opening act, subordinates aligned simply to warm up the crowd.

The tango ensemble hadn't even so much as nodded a greeting the entire night, and Nat had noticed the snub. Though mindful that they had played well over their time, Nat felt he owed no apologies as he bent down to look closely upon the group, an ensemble outfitted in matching gold-stretch sequined swallowtail suits, black lapels, and maroon bow ties. With his arm extended, Nat blew out the lyrics in their direction, playfully piquing their rancorous attitude.

The intense writhe in their faces was hardly necessary, giving away an obvious fact to Nat that they had just finished a session of cocaine bumps in the bathroom moments before, wanting the stage before their highs subsided into a need for more. Brows were furrowed over dilated pupils. Jaw muscles flexed relentlessly. A thumb was drawn across a running nose. Recognizing the state of this group, Nat felt justified to sing on as they spastically rocked side to side in aggrieved madness.

The song ended to the exclamatory praise of the room, though not from the new patrons but the young throng of Brix and Styx, who thoroughly celebrated the volume, the way it made the exclusive stiffs shrink.

"Thank you, Denver! Now don't forget to stick around for . . . for . . ." Making sure the mic was close to his mouth, Nat leaned down to the one who appeared to be the band leader, "What was your name again?"

In response came an all-too-distinguishable assertion of anger at the inquiry, as the Don Juan doppelganger, who appeared to be the lead man, folded his arms across his ruffled white tuxedo shirt, mouthing the words "fuck you."

Alive and Well paid them no mind as they broke down their gear. Only Dolf remained seated behind his kit. Despite giving in to his beckon to play longer than normal another time, it wasn't enough, as he broke into a solo, startling his mates, freezing them.

The band in wait advanced to the stage and jumped atop it, parking in front of Dolf, daring him to play on. Moby, Nat, and Baker were quick to shadow the angry group, ready to support their drummer, regardless of the fact they strongly opposed the stunt he was pulling.

Dolf looked at the five incensed faces and grinned, playing harder and harder on his snare. He stood up to leave his bass pedal, rising a good two inches over the tallest of his challengers, smirking at their absurd mustaches, which had been painted on to lend a look of debonair showmanship. He started a run on his toms and, with a quick transition, beat a riff across the white fedora of the one standing within reach. Dolf's wrist was grabbed with a catlike reflex, the result of being so brazenly humiliated.

And he would not let go, squeezing harder. A beat continued with one hand, Dolf grinned, and the holder of the drummer's arm began to regret his decision. Dolf pulled back with such force that the foe was sent flying over his drums, to land well behind him, ending wrapped up in the curtain backdrop, his fedora lying across his hunched backside like a Velveteen ghost. Even though Dolf had just thrown a man several feet through the air, he never lost the tempo, maintaining a soft beat on his ping ride while returning his other hand to point a wary stick at the others.

Baker was promptly at his shoulder. "Easy, man. That's enough."

The cymbal faded out, but Dolf did not leave his post immediately, daring any other brave soul to try their luck.

And Moby came to the other side, bookending his drummer, trying to settle him. "C'mon now, bruh, don't blow it. Don't ruin the performance on these guys."

Dolf turned to Moby, breathing out his flared nose like a raging bull. At last, he slowly set his sticks down on his stool and started to twist his toms free from the set, keeping one eye set on his perceived enemy, as Moby gave his own wary eye to the chic ensemble. "Give us a sec. Then you Panama Jacks can have the stage."

Dolf zipped the last of his gear. He bent down to grab one case under each arm. And as he turned his attention away from his new adversaries, he received one last earful. "Hey, shit for brains, don't think for a second that you'll ever make it in this business, you hear me, fool!"

Moby had been in charge of Dolf for the time being but had taken his bass to the back of the room, committing the horrible mistake of leaving his drummer alone. Dolf dropped what he was doing to face the one of such brassy nerve. The most stout of the five stood out from the others. Whether it was he who uttered the remark or not, the outrageous-looking musketeer stood primed for retaliation.

To know Dolf was to know his strategy. An initial punch to the nose usually ended any fracas quickly. If not, it caused the adversary's eyes to well up with tears enough to finish the job. Tonight's rival had a stately proboscis, like Cyrano de Bergerac. Surely, he was proud of it. And with one straight-on jab to the protruding target, Dolf left the musician on his knees, bleeding and broken. That was that.

The audience sat in silence, observing the showdown as if it were a main event on a fight card, Bruno the Cavalier versus Dolf the Pissed. Nat and Baker were dodging chairs on their way back to intercept the confrontation but froze in midstride when they saw Dolf swing, dropping their heads, feeling their hearts hit the floor.

At the back of the room, Lorenzo's mouth had fallen open in utter amazement. Not since his days as a young boy had he seen such anger. Nina swore she could feel the rage from where she sat as well. Any words were lost amid the goings-on, and the uncomfortable hush prompted Nina to spur things along. "I don't know about you, baby, but I'm goin' to the car."

But Lorenzo felt sympathetic to the other members of Alive and Well. He desired to remain for a while, to see how it would all turn out. He escorted Nina to the car, handing her the keys. "Why don't you warm it up, baby. I'll be back in just a few."

Alive and Well packed the trailer up in a long-rehearsed method, without a word. There was nothing that could come out of anyone's mouth to dispel what had happened. Compliments on the gig would be moot points. Rebukes to its aftermath were futile, leaving nothing to do but roll home and sleep it off.

But Jimmy stormed out of Club Nomad at a high speed, the expression on his face telling the others that he would not be going so quietly. They all rose to sluggish attention on his arrival—all but Dolf, who kept his head within the trailer, stacking and restacking cabinets without purpose.

"I just had a severely one-sided conversation with the manager!" said Jimmy in a high-pitched inflection of fury. "And guess what. We're not allowed to show our faces in this establishment ever again. Imagine that. What's this make now, two, no, three venues that we can just kiss goodbye. At this rate, we'll be left with playin' tent revivals for trite blessings for the rest of our existence!"

Jimmy jabbed a finger into Dolf's shoulder. "Hey, I got news for you, old buddy. You're outta here! You hear me? You are so fired that I'd kick your butt up the street if I weren't so damn afraid of you. Now get out of here and leave us the hell alone!"

No immediate words came from Baker, quietly crushed at what had transpired before him. His leadership was orated by Jimmy in words he could never use but in an opinion he couldn't help but side with. He only looked down to his swollen fingers, which tapped incessantly on the pill bottle in his pocket. After putting the one-two antidote of Tolectin and Demerol on his tongue, he swallowed hard. With no retort from their leader, Moby, Nat, and Murphy stepped aside as well.

Dolf pushed away from the doors, closing them ever so gently like he was closing this chapter of his life, which was his favorite.

"Dolf . . . hey . . . lemme get you home," pleaded Baker, walking after his friend. "We can talk about this . . . get you some help." Baker reached out, took Dolf by the arm.

Dolf pulled away with aggression. "Look, Bake. Don't touch me. I'm warning you."

It wasn't what came from his mouth but what was said in his eyes. They were crazy wild. Baker couldn't tell if it was rage or fear, or both. The next move needed to be a careful one.

He stood in front of his friend, at least the husk of him. Baker felt Dolf falling into the next level of his mania. There would be no reaching him.

Moby had approached, putting his hand on Baker's shoulder. "C'mon, bruh. Nothing we can do tonight." Moving Baker behind him, Moby looked into the depths of Dolf's wild stare, and after two beats, Dolf's gaze fell on Moby.

"Be careful out there, Dolf . . . and next time you see us, it's my turn for a game of chess. Got it?"

For the first time, the contest did not illicit a response, not so much as a flinch in his stone expression. Without looking back, he walked off, in what seemed to be slow motion, across the street, fading into the cobalt night.

This night was a rare occasion where no one could find the energy to worry about what he could do to himself. Even if, later, calmer heads prevailed, no one knew where Dolf would go, or if they would ever see him again.

Their stamina was on empty. Only Jimmy, of such diminutive stature in both the mental and the physical, had the wherewithal to do what had to be done. Of the five who had comprised Alive and Well, he maintained a companionship the farthest toward the fringe, far enough away to finally deliver the final consequence to Dolf's temper with the ultimate penalty. No telling how long it would have taken the others to hit the switch. Baker, Nat, Moby, and Murphy each stared into the pavement, feeling the onerous guilt of being grateful for what Jimmy had done.

Lorenzo didn't smoke cigarettes any more. But he had bummed one in order to go outside and puff on it, pretending to mind his own business and bear witness to the hammer being brought down on the band's drummer. They looked so tired in his eyes—innocent, bewildered at the predicament of being outcasts in a pursuit they poured their souls into with such unconditional disregard. He appreciated the band's sound and felt regret for what they were going through. He wanted to praise them on their absolute talents, for he felt connected, once being lost himself in such a morass of uncertainty.

It wouldn't be until later that night, while lying awake in bed beside his adorable sleeping Nina, looking out the window into the winter's night, that he clearly envisioned the possibilities. They may just fold up their tents, quit, he thought. But turning back upon the evening, he remembered the look on the guitarist's face as he played, realizing there was no way that guy could ever let this setback end everything. His expressions read plainly the telling story of what he was born to do, what he *had* to do.

Lorenzo felt he had something to offer, seeing clearly that he could help turn that group into something special. They wouldn't have to worry about him. The restraints could be dropped, leaving the singer to wail at will, the bassist to pluck freely, the guitarist to play like he did to those crackerjack drummers who radiated from his earphones at home.

He would find them again, maybe from a beckoning advertisement:

> *DRUMMER NEEDED. Experienced with an ability to learn an unconventional style. Able to handle multiple changeovers mid-song, control the posi-tion with no handholding. If into drugs and alcohol, don't bother. SERIOUS INQUIRIES ONLY! Yours in Christ,*
> *ALIVE AND WELL*

11

ANOTHER STATISTIC

Acockroach lumbered slowly across a matted burnt-orange shag carpet, stopping just in time to flick out its antennae, avoid his boot. Dolf watched its lackluster escape, bouncing over the dingy pile. "You're easy to stomp," he said in a slur to the bug. "The German roach, on the other hand, now he's a speedster— must be quick. But you of the Oriental variety, you, my friend, are no match." As Dolf raised his boot to smash the bug, it stopped, turned, flicking its feelers as if sending Morse code.

I feel your tendency to snuff me out. You bemused soul, what did I ever do to you?

The carpet changed its color to a rusty obsidian. The muscle in Dolf's jaw flexed. The voice of the insect was Asian, like James Hong.

"I suppose my state of mind gives me the excuse to do so," answered Dolf.

So do it, Big Drummerboy. Yeah. I know you, the under-qualified and overwhelmed one.

"Hey, now . . ."

You wanted immediate gratification, you nincompoop. The frequency of success. Now look at you.

Dolf began to feel the heat rise on his neck.

You feel God has apportioned out his gifts unevenly, and you wanna take it out on me, eh? A poor bug.

The roach twilled his antennae at the ends, affecting a pose that his dukes were up. *Well c'mon then, assuage your mind with violence in this, this den of violence.*

Dolf exhaled deeply. Sweat began to bead on his brow. He leaned back, turning to his right hand that spun a .38 Special around the table, which ended up, more times than not, pointing at his chest. The ashtray was already half full.

He had almost made it home. Dolf stood stock-still at the intersection of Eleventh and Pearl, across the street from his apartment. He punched himself hard in the arm, in the face, in an attempt to release enough endorphins to ease the chaos, sneak by the terror and confusion and into his building. But in front of him had lurked a barricade of haunting impressions. Shadows slid along walls that breathed; insects covered the sidewalk and began spilling into the street, toward him. And such images provoked him to keep walking, fast.

Estranged now from Alive and Well, from his friends and the personal therapy of music, Dolf felt his anger being replaced by a gut-wrenching sadness as he took to the middle of the street. His tangled mind filled more with shame with each step away from his apartment, a fatal mood to which he drunkenly zigzagged to avoid. Several blocks later, Dolf lost the feeling in his toes. Exhausted and cold, he approached a light that was on in the front window of a motel, North End Inn. The neon bulbs that still worked flickered against the chill of the night, blinking crazily to display only the last two words, "End Inn."

The night manager appeared behind muddy bulletproof glass. Other than a silhouette confirming a short and plump form, his appearance was indecipherable. As he slid out a metal drawer, his pitch came through an intercom in a low and croaky voice, "Twenty bucks. No matter if you're stayin' twenty minutes or the night. Twenty bucks."

Dolf pressed the bill into the drawer. It snapped closed, catching his numb fingertips. In return came a key on a plastic tag, "#9." "You're out by noon, got it?"

He was cornered by all the characteristics he had avoided with such care. And now Dolf sat at the edge of a soiled motel bed, in the dead calm of the dead of night, with not enough alcohol to drink himself to sleep. No television could distract him. It had likely been stolen, as only the cable wire poked out from the wall, levitating two inches above the dresser. Through his blurred faculties, Dolf was sure he saw it move ever so slightly in his direction, like a microphone repositioned by the people in the next room.

"What do you want!" he hollered, resonant, arresting. " Come'eer. I got something for ya!"

The plastic pint of whiskey went to his lips, turned up almost vertical until the last drop hit his chin. If the clock was accurate, it was 3:35. No matter, the darkness and the quiet knew the occasion, another opportunity to tear into this man, who mumbled on, throwing disjointed bromides out like spears at the beast that sat smugly savage in the corner. It looked to almost smile at Dolf, flashing its sharp yellow teeth, furling and unfurling its black leather wings, waiting patiently for its prey, for the stream of consciousness to run dry.

You know that big dog over there? The one you're trying so hard to ignore? It's never cared much for your bravado. And your currency, what was in that bottle there, evidently has run dry. Soooo. You gonna give it up, or what?

The band was lost. And Dolf's heart ached at the thought. From the sorrow grew hostility, and the beast's tongue rolled out between its teeth. The glint from the light of the parking lot on the revolver enticed Dolf to pick it up.

Look at you. You're not fit for this. You're incapable of housing a human spirit.

Dolf lowered his head, and it swirled, reaching for the thinnest strands of cognitive thought, to tie them together, and survive another night. *Baker. I need Baker's faith. I need to pray.*

The cockroach pushed him further.

Ahhh. Silly fool. You're searching for something. This manner of a heretic in front of me is looking for help.

"God, I . . . I . . . need you," Dolf whispered, low enough so as not to let the bug hear. To no avail, the cockroach heard everything.

God? Your god has no compassion. He is a god of vengeance. He is of a stone heart, he is. A barren one indeed . . . and he's had it with you.

"Lord, my silence is the loudest. Baker has shown me the knowledge to know you are beside me. Please . . . please quiet my mind."

Yes. Yes, Lord. Quiet his paper-thin mind. The world will continue to spin without you walking all over it. End this now. No witnesses. A clean break.

Dolf's mind broke in two directions, one directing his hand to put the gun to his temple, the other instructing him to recite the Lord's Prayer. The barrel was pressed deep against his brain as Dolf recollected recent deeds from his life, impulsive acts that cut his tether, leaving him to fly outside the arc of a moral universe.

Beliefs are so esoteric, Dolf. Pull the trigger.

"Thy kingdom come, thy will be done."

Faith is in the abstract. Pull the trigger.

"Forgive us our trespasses."

Jesus on the cross. That's gruesome. Pull the trigger.

"Deliver us from evil."

With that, the door swung open to the most brilliant light. Dolf was unfazed as he continued into the deepest prayer of his life. But the cockroach twitched to the intrusion, dropping his antennae to the familiar face, just letting out an "aw, man" before his thorax hit the wall with a pop.

A beast growled and then yelped. And one gunshot rang out in the night.

The police got the call. With no lights flashing, no sirens blaring, the black-and-white made its way into the motel driveway thirty minutes after dispatch. Finding the proprietor drunk and unconscious behind the lobby glass, the two officers shook him awake.

After keying the door, the slumlord groped his way back to his confines, closing his door and his care of the situation.

A man was found sitting in the middle of the room, his head tilted straight back at a right angle from his shoulders. The gun had dropped from his dangling arm and sat in a dark pool, splashed in deep burgundy from the flow of his head, the blood running down the arm, dripping from his fingertips.

The two officers approached, unemotional, for this kind of thing happened all the time in this neck of the woods. The "Inglorious Inn," as it was called at the station, was good for no more than housing cheap hookers, heroin addicts, and people like this, the defeated, resting at their last stop on the road to nowhere. They flipped to see who would do the paperwork.

Continuing with lackluster, they surveyed the scene. Avoiding the mess, they stood back, arms folded, figuring in quick cohesion that foul play was of no consideration. To investigate further would just be wasted effort.

There was a time when the vulgarity and brutality got to them. But a certain degree of detachment was requisite. The ethos: "To Protect and to Serve." But there was no one left to save here. So the pace was slow, not meticulous. It was simply cold outside, and the suicide served as a morbid break to the evening. The men in blue called it in, stood in the center of the room, touching nothing. Here, there was no chance to make a difference. In a place where the sleaze slid downhill to land, this man in the chair had chosen to end his situational misery in shame, in the dark. The officers stood silent, hoping he had no wife, no close family left on hands and knees, to pick up the pieces.

Snow was caught in a gust, swirling upward into the beam of an arc lamp at Eleventh and Pearl, Capitol Hill. Five men had left their cars and stood under the light, as the light lent a false sense that it was warmer there. They had driven the neighborhood most of the night, looking for any sign of their friend. His apartment was across the street. But Dolf had never come home. All they could do was wait, and pray he had not left the gig to find a bottle and pass out cold in weather so frigid that it had cleared the streets of partygoers and vagrants hours ago. Moby smoked as the others rocked from one foot to the other, hands jammed in pockets for relief from the temperature. No one spoke. With minds enclosed in worry, they had simply run out of things to say, mulling a conclusion that would change their lives forever.

As Moby threw his cigarette on the sidewalk, he noticed footprints in the snow that were not theirs. "Look," he said, pointing down.

Murphy squatted down to study the imprint. "That's a big shoe."

"It's him," determined Baker almost instantly. "Look at the tread, diamonds, straight lines on the front and back. It's a Chuck Taylor. Who wears canvass Chuck Taylor's in this weather?"

The tracks left the corner and proceeded up Eleventh Street. They followed the path as it meandered into the middle of the street. Suddenly, the late-night moan of a city in slumber was broken by a distant crack. Toward its direction they walked, north, in an area where graffiti flourished into a run-on dialect from building to building, where plywood covered more windows than glass, where liquor stores operated on every third corner and empty churches crumbled.

Baker was thrust back to a moment in time he had endeavored to put on the highest shelf, so as to be unable to reach it. Though, he knew his subconscious was not a vault but a mere doorway, unaligned so as to be stuck yet accessible with the right amount of force. And such an overt sound as a shot in the night had wrenched the memory free once again, bringing forth a melancholy realization that he could never truly remove the blemish on his soul. The bleakest episode of his life would remain a stigma, a massive and crude stain in his mind only turned inside out in an attempt to hide from the outside world.

Suddenly, wind-displaced snow hit Baker and the others head-on. His friends turned away from the blast while Baker leaned into it, allowing the raw chill to break the hold of his desolate thoughts and rebel against them. Discouragement faded. Rather than resolve to accept a fate yet unknown, Baker breathed deeply. He rolled his shoulders, cocked is head gently left and right, and reached deep into his soul. Exalted against a punishing hopelessness, Baker reached out to connect in spirit with his missing friend. He no longer felt the cold but the warming awareness that a higher power was at hand. And a feeling of imaginary wanton satisfaction became palpably likely under the growing confidence he was not alone.

Baker was only brought out of his rapture by a vibration that emanated from his coat pocket. He reached in to pull out his phone, and the glow illuminated his face as he lifted his head to the pitch-dark sky in relief at who was on the other end.

ACKNOWLEDGMENTS

I want to thank my wife, whom I love with all my heart, for growing in Christ with me and loving me unconditionally through our life together. Thank you for wearing so many hats for our family, allowing me to pursue this unconventional dream.

To my amazing children, who make me so proud every day, I'm honored to be your father and look forward to seeing the mark you make on this world.

Audra, thank you for your tremendous skills and insight to make this story shine brighter. My humble gratitude to everyone who read my story, especially when it wasn't ready for prime time, yet gave me the impression that I had done something special. And Mom and Dad, always supportive and patient during a kid's life full of wrong moves, you allowed me to fail enough to learn from it, and I found the education to be irreplaceable. I love you both.

Waverly gets the credit for the lyrics Nat sings from the stage—and, along with Aaron, Eric, Beau, Mike, and Charlie, gave me the bones to characters I could flesh out in fiction. As well, thanks to Disciple for allowing me to use some lyrics from "3, 2, 1." B.A. desperately needed that song to launch his sermon. And to all the performers who evangelize through music, this story is for you all. The notes you play, the words you make, provide more than a song. Your message helps so many people, especially the young, helping them to get through the rough patches of life. Your grace saves, and I feel privileged to have met so many of you along the way.

Finally, "Cheers" to the Bigger Crew. You're always there, making me laugh every day, without fail. I'm blessed to have you all as friends.

And of course, to my Lord and Savior. The blessings bestowed upon me are hard to reconcile, given the misdeeds in my life. But You love me unconditionally, as You love us all.

Just turn around and He's there, without fail.

ABOUT THE AUTHOR

G.K. last darkened the church door at eight years old. Morally adrift, the author led an iconoclastic life of self-gratification, depriving himself of virtually nothing.

Embraced in heavy drinking and recreational drugs as a young man, his writing career bounced half-deflated through fly-by-night publications, from a dive bar reviews to a quixotic travel column, from a music critic to landing as a published roaster of professional athletes, always finding an easy landing through criticism, as disparaging remarks came easily. Then something changed. Marriage happened, three children ensued, and God reappeared.

By His Grace, G.K. spun the wheel away from former habits and composed the first part of a fictional story, applying dashes of personal experience, hoping to glorify the Heavenly Father through good works now and in the years to come.